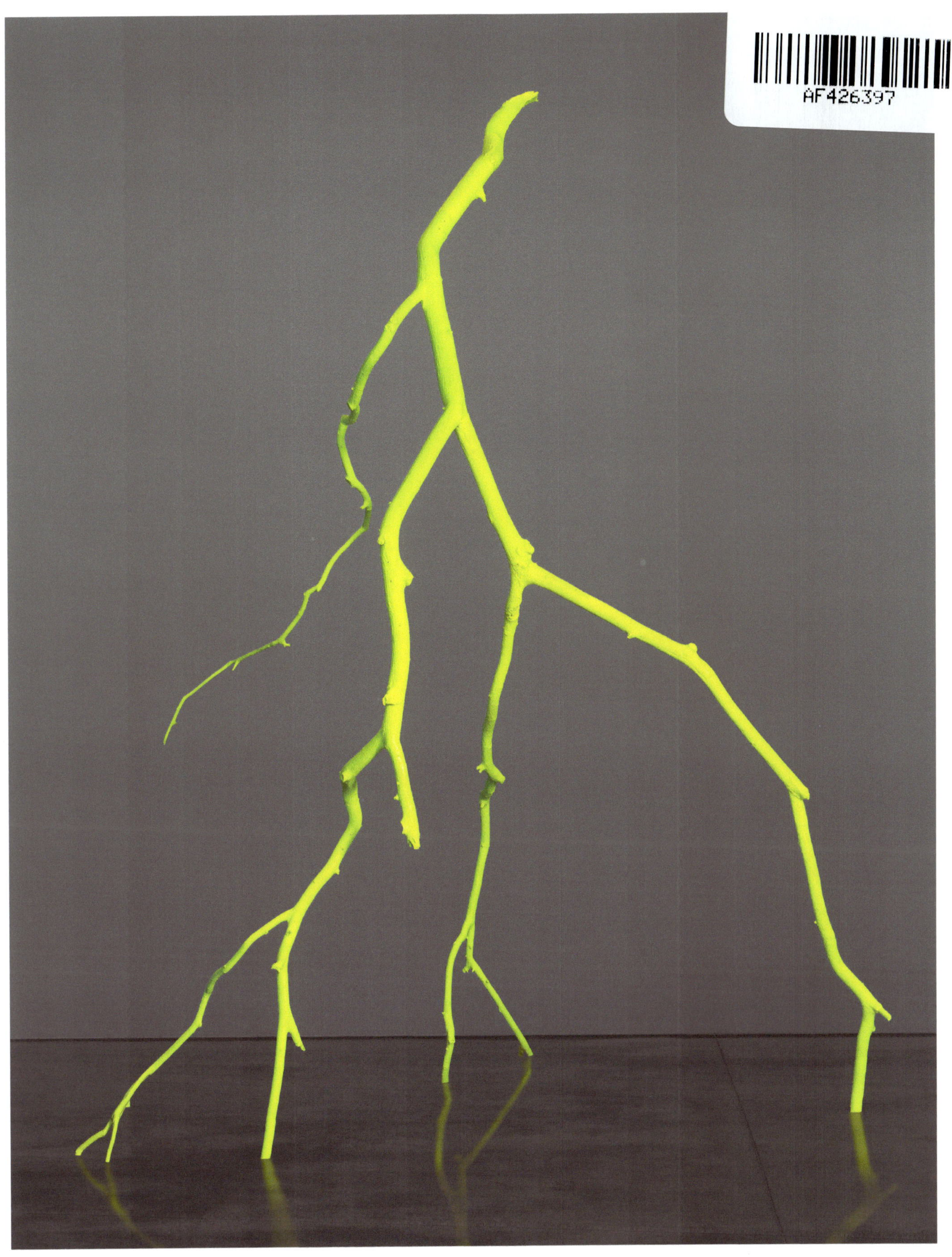

sublime light , 2023, © Ugo Rondinone, courtesy of the artist and Gladstone Gallery
Painted bronze, 242 1/2 x 146 5/8 x 132 1/4 in. (616 x 372.2 x 335.7 cm)

Rick Prol

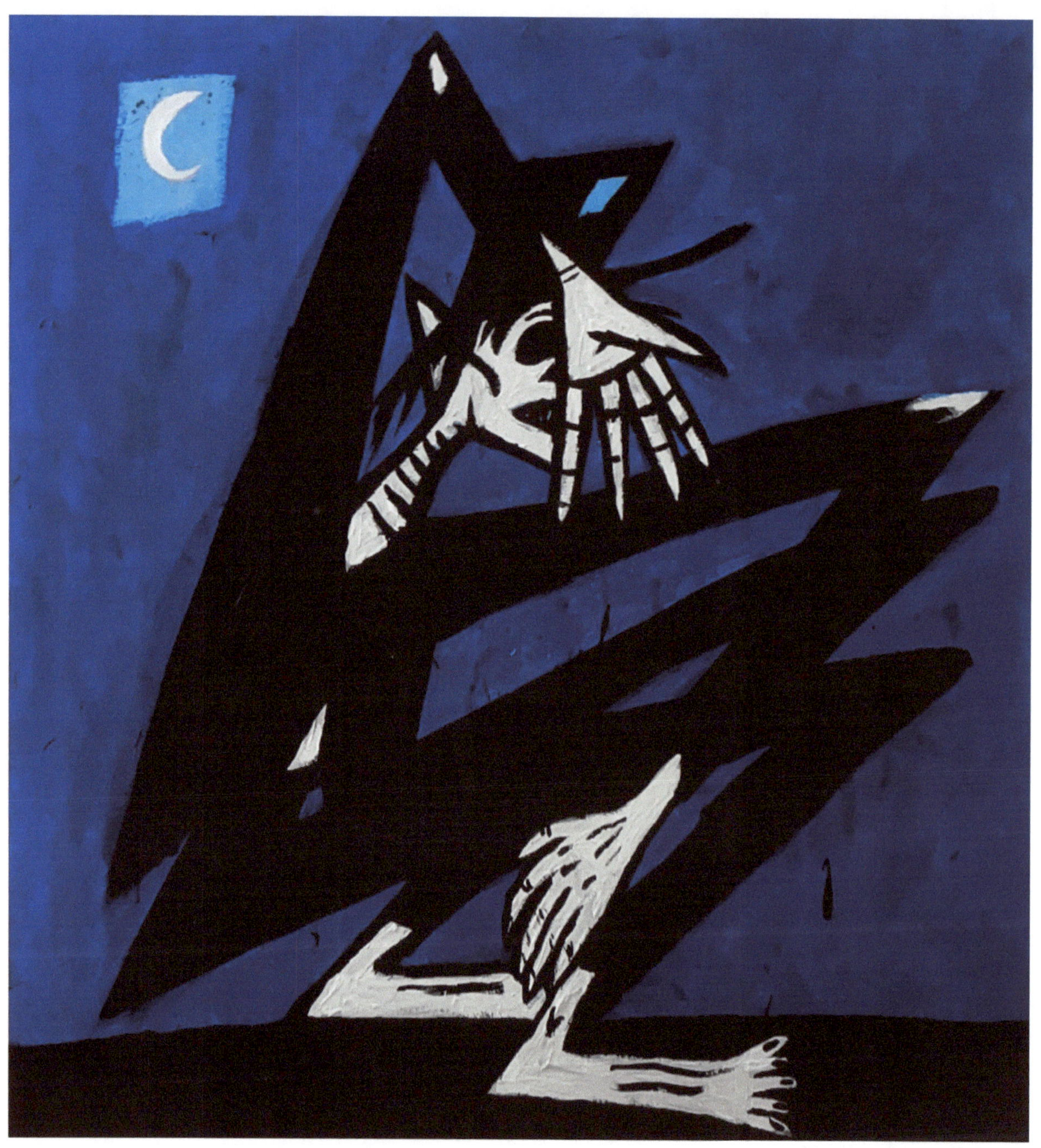

Peek A Boo, 2023, acrylic on canvas, 36 x 34 in.
Courtesy James Fuentes and Michael Klein and the artist

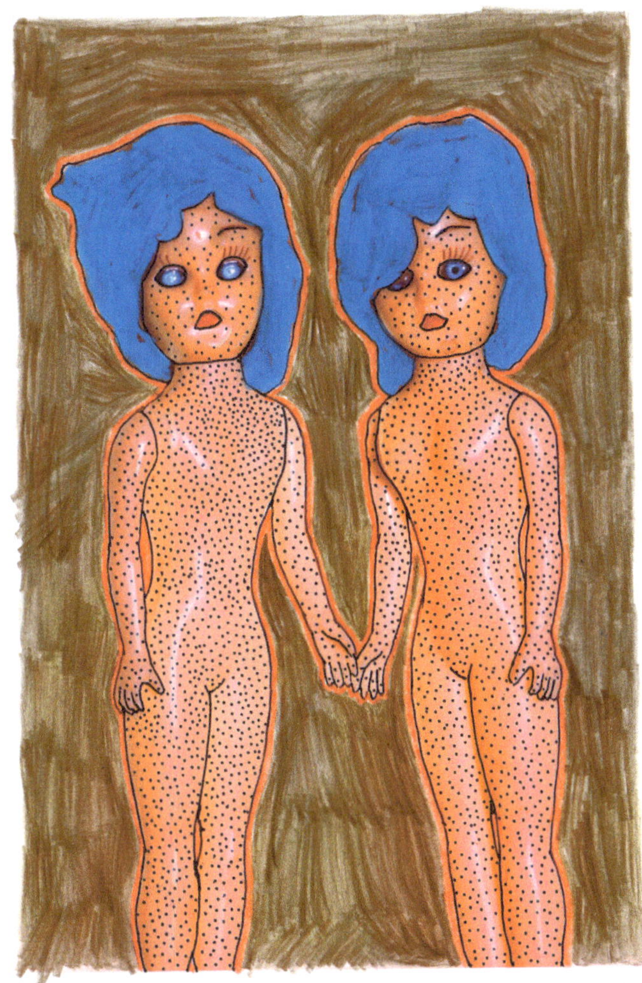

Marcia Resnick, *Two Girls with Blue Hair and Blue Eyes*, 2018. Archival pigment print with applied oil paint. Paper 10 x 8" titled in ink in margin recto, signed, dated & annotated #1 in pencil on verso. Copyright © Marcia Resnick, courtesy Deborah Bell Photographs, New York and Paul M. Hertzmann, Inc., San Francisco.

Publisher and Editor: Jeffrey Cyphers Wright
Deputy Editor: Ilka Scobie
Associate Editor: Lori Ortiz
Cover art: JCW; Design: LO
©2024 Live Mag!
Box 1215 Cooper Station, NY NY 10276
https://livemag.org **SUBSCRIBE!**

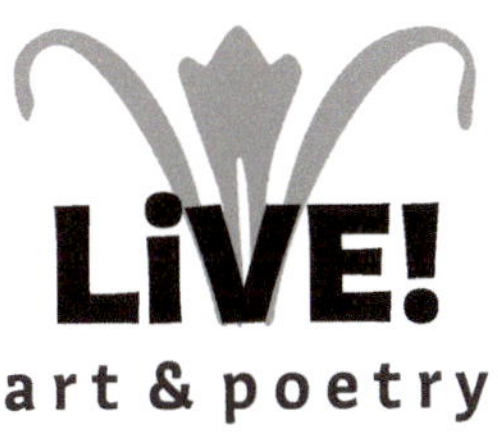

Ed Sanders

A STABBING LEADS TO A LIFE-LONG RELATIONSHIP

In the A.M. of January 7, 1938
Samuel Beckett was stabbed by someone
demanding money, & Beckett saying No
on a Paris street

The knife missed the heart
from the waddings of his coat
though it could have killed him

A young woman named
Suzanne Deschevaux-Dumesnil
returning from a concert
came to Sam's distress
wrapped him in a friend's overcoat
& swathed together a pillow 'neath
his head, then called for an ambulance

He was taken to a hospital
where he was saved

James Joyce loaned him a reading lamp
during his stay in the hospital

& Beckett corrected the proofs of *Murphy.*

He was discharged from l' hôpital on 1-23-38

And as for Suzanne the Savior — she was a
skilled pianist & teacher of piano
& for the next decades served Sam,
while fiercely protecting herself from the public
as she "moved into his life."

In World War II living with Suzanne
  Sam stored dynamite
            for the Resistance
                    in his house.

& so it went on unto the always.

THE PREMIERE OF WAITING FOR GODOT IN 1953

Late in the year his mate Suzanne brought
"Waiting for Godot"
to producer Roger Blin, who read it w/ care
in part because Tristan Tzara
   had praised Beckett —

Blin soon agreed to put it on.

There was trouble locating a Theater
Finally Blin secured the tiny
Théâtre de Babylone

for an opening January 5, 1953

Godot had only four actors, in low-income
costumery, so they could wear their street clothes

& Blin wouldn't need much illumination
beyond a spotlight & a barren tree on the stage.

Beckett attended rehearsals & work-ups,
hesitating at first to butt in
because of his lack of experience
    in Theater
but soon he began to shape the acting
& stage-business (and always thereafter)
& took great charge of Godot
  & all future plays
   & scripts.

The opening was shouted to the rafters
& suddenly, at 47, Sam was famous

Chris Martin

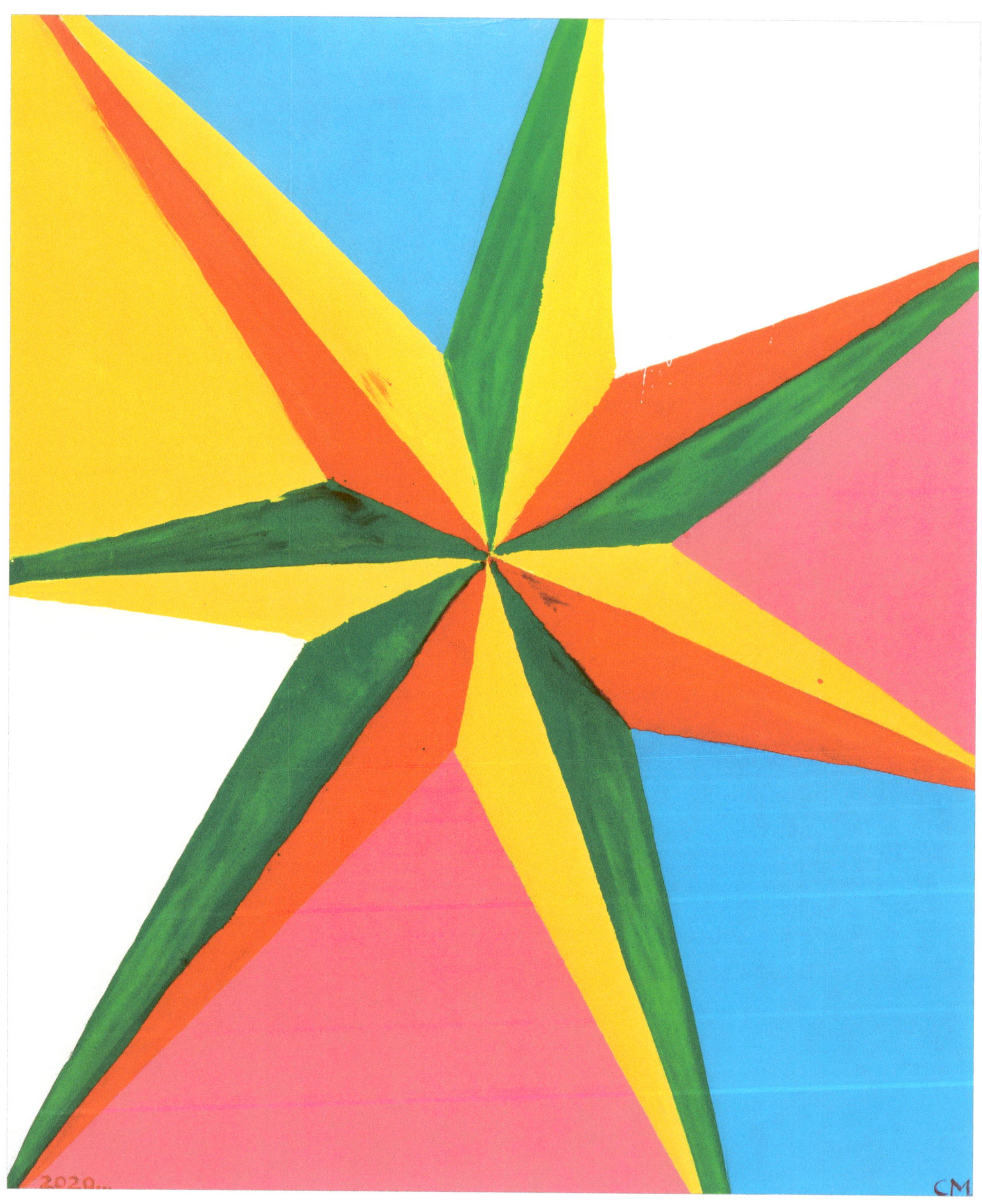

Seven Pointed Star for LA, 2020, acrylic on canvas, 75 x 64 in.
Courtesy of Eric Firestone Gallery.

Gingerbread House

It was not exactly a house,
more a large room at the end of a path
dotted with cupcakes and birds
where she lived with someone
like a brother you could sleep with
because that's what the story called for.

There was also a witch, at least
the rumor of one, who rarely visited
because she was busy doing
witches' work in the larger forest.
The witch did not have to do much
to keep them in the gingerbread guesthouse.
They were free to leave at any time,
but chose not to — preferring to bake
and take care of the cat.

Every day the girl was grateful to her father
for having abandoned her.

TITLES ONLY

Be, Hear, Now
The Earth Is a Drum We Walk On
Our Lady of Opaque
Neither Fiction, Nor Fact
Winsome, Lose Some
The Pep Police
Haiku Handcuffs
A Leopard Doesn't Change Its Stripes

Give It a Try

Bring nothing.
A goddess on a bank of roses waits for you.
Let the rocks and water of a hidden spring
sedate you with their music.
You were here long ago, perhaps
in another life. Who knows?
Who should know?
Banish clothes, reenter the water,
embrace the moment. Remember?
The night grows lovely with moonglow.
Don't ask why.
The world outside is beautiful
but broken in many places.
People have turned sticks and stones
into missiles and bombs,
other gadgets of self-destruction.
They have turned green into brown.
Domes of fire halo their heads.
Lies haunt their speech.
It is cool where you are.
A forest of love surrounds you.
Time is that moment you forgot.
Imagination is eternal.
Give it a try.

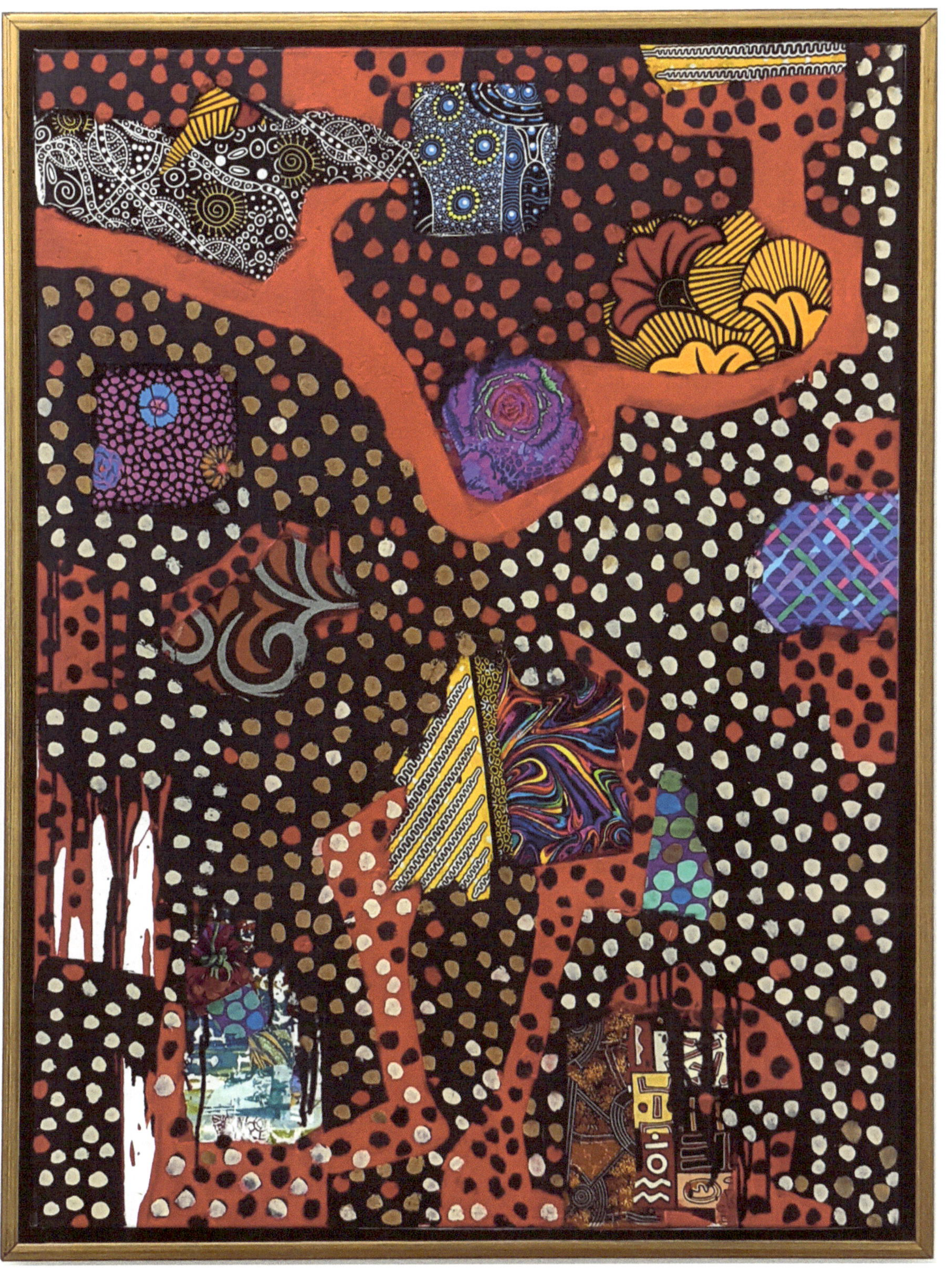

Tribes Of NY, 2021, oil and fabric on canvas, 40 x 30 in | 101.6 x 76.2 cm.
Courtesy the artist and Westwood Gallery NYC.

Isabel Muñoz

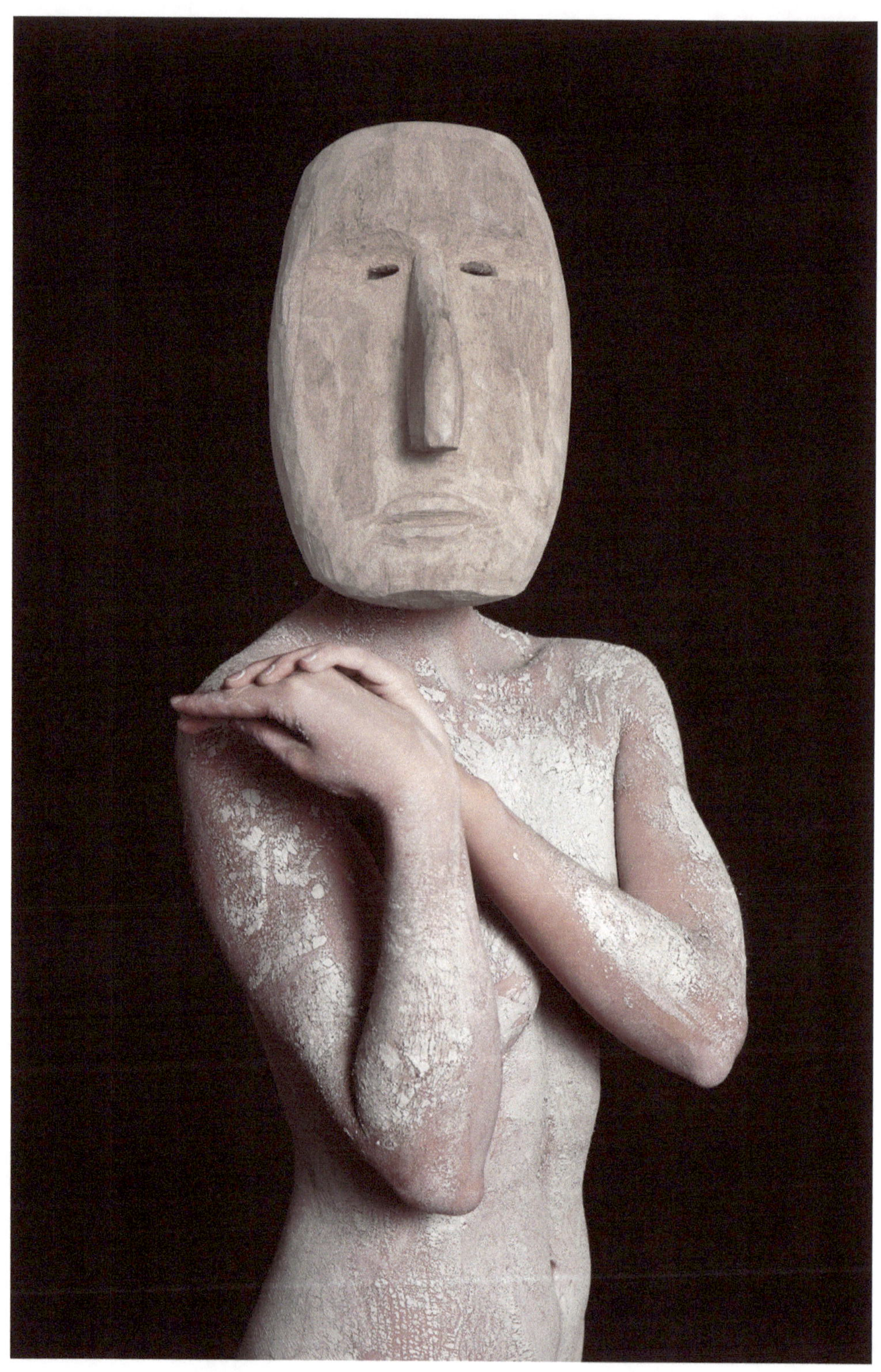

MIT 0806, 2023. Color platinum print, 31½ x23¾ in.
Courtesy of Throckmorton Gallery.

Wanda Phipps

Response to "if I am not being killed" by Ukrainian poet Iryna Shuvalova

what right do I have to speak
to you when your homes
are being bombed
when I am safe and war

what right do I have
to speak to you
when I see the photos
and the footage on TV
of buildings blown apart
of women and children
covered in blood
lying in rubble
carried on stretchers
and I feel a heavy boot
stomping on my chest
my hands going numb
my throat tightening
so much I couldn't
speak if I wanted to

I'm not in danger
but it feels like we all are
we all will be
the threat
the pain
the loss
seeps through
all the cracks
of complacency

we speak the same language
as sure as blood is red
and hearts can break

Nicole Eisenman

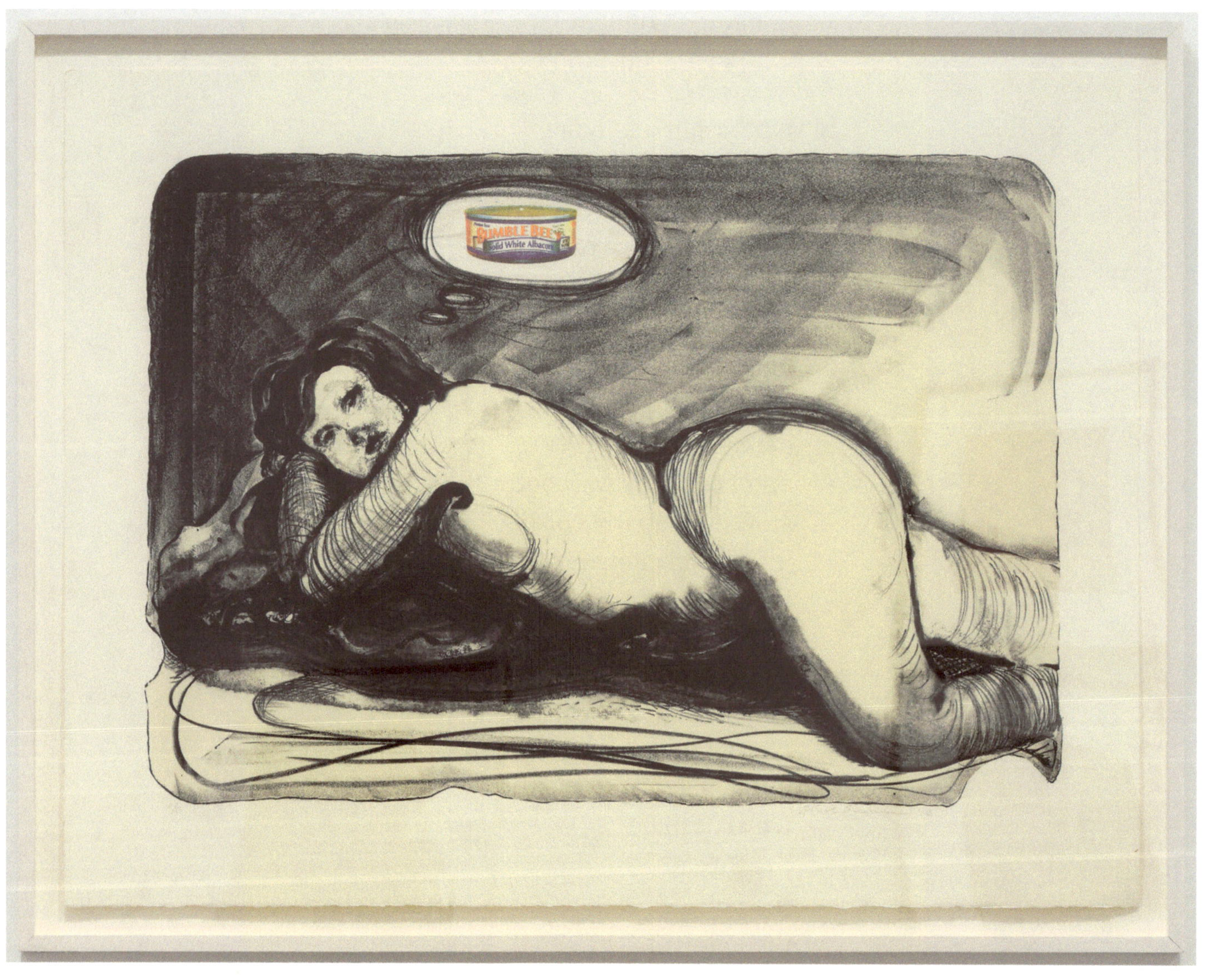

The Thinker, 2012, lithograph print, 25 x 33¼ in.
Edition of 25 by Jungle Press Editions, Courtesy Jungle Press Editions. © Nicole Eisenman.
Photo by Argenis Apolinario for Print Center New York.

Ballerina Boy

a disarming investigator partial to daring leaps
a paycheck
steady lines of each welfare state
like in Massachusetts
either 15 or 50
you lived a lot
on some of the best stages:
Garnier, Metropolitan, Berliner Schauspielhaus
getting used to a stretch of time
hairpin turns
fashion
youth
let him be him
keeping up the façade
until the assumptions held him accountable
"Afternoon of a Faun"
with Frank O'Hara and Edwin Denby
the lost intimacy cracking
under a mackerel sky
the artistic leisure glimmering through eras
swords of terrifying light
breaking both ears
both feet both eyes both nostrils
a cloud of phlegm
an octopus ranging through a salty wet skull
looking more toward where fingertips
guide the core
engaged
with tears
streaming across the dreaming courage

Georgia Pavlidou

Anti-lamps

for Adam Cornford

a
i'm a floating
compound ghost
of night-crows

i operate
on sleepless
turquoise & trazadone

flocks of unamerican ur-birds
seeking photosynthesis at night,
are after me

"you're our aleph, tau, theta & phi,"
they're cawing flying behind me
"please devour our anti-lamps."

b
in kindergarten-universities
indigo-leprechauns are sketching
my contours

"the outer edges have to be narrower
than her volume," they say

"she's our phi,
our sexless salamander
in constant anti-copulation

raised
in two unrelated foreign languages
she hatches under haunted glass

confiscate her anti-lamps"

c
"during the day she's accused
of having white privilege

at dusk
she becomes an admirador of sorrow,
scavenging for moon-hurt &
the opposite of metamorphosis

indigo-leprechauns love this

pawn your anti-lamps"

d
an inferior race
of famished mental carnivores
agreed to adopt an anti-lamp

selling isolation & turquoise
at dark-blue prices
is their core business

"its hellenic letters
will help us expand,"
they claim

"we're proud of our
admiradores of human sorrow"

e
in india you cannot
not have a religion

in india you cannot
not have a caste

in india
damnation in the blue hellfire
of identity is eternal

& here's the thing:

indigo-parents
often praise the
turquoise overlords
that enslaved
their barely-blue
ancestors

devour ten bags of spicy anti-lamps

f
do you believe in spirit-doubles?
well, in last night's dreaming

my blue spirit-double & i
waltzed on gigantic triangles of turquoise

while slinging anti-lamps

g
barely round circles
tried swallowing up my contours

"back off," an indigo-leprechaun said,

"you're too new to watch triangles & circles
  copulate,

your eyes will catch fire."

hearing this
my burning eyeballs instantly
visualized barely round circles

devouring my anti-lamps

h
it's the 4th of July, &
indigo-leprechauns running kindergarten-universities
haven't stopped visualizing my contours

their heads mutter:

"somebody is sketching you into existence,
 somebody is sketching you out of existence"

yet my blue spirit-double & I,
we're still waltzing on enormous
turquoise triangles

slinging anti-lamps at great velocity

i
swallowed up
my own contours,

i've exited the floating compound
ghost of night-crows

hunting for photosynthesis at night
a sad ur-bird
caught me & said:

"you're my aleph, tau, theta & phi"

but i devoured all its anti-lamps."

indigo-leprechauns love this

Joel Dailey

CLING TO THE NOTION

She's a good day to dilate she's
A day for fisticuffs
Out There pandemic wingnuts spawn conspiracy lies out
What's left of the wazoo
In fact the new currency is toilet tissue
(I think I believe
I possibly may
have an ear infuckshun)
Which leads to my plan for World Domination which
May be thwarted
Upended
Or calmly brushed aside
By a baby carriage descending a staircase by
A fat cell burning contest
Or by vociferous consumption of genuine embossed Infodemic geegaws
(ultra-violent rays
are heartfelt
against the green felt)
But wait
Far beyond the 6 foot social distancing Arc de Triomphe this canned gravy sucks
In tandem I have wasted my mashed potatoes in
A field strewn with horse

RUBBER EAR

Woke up just now in a shack on Typewriter Key, Florida
The clairvoyants did not see the crosstown bus
You are on the verge of something huge
My tricks play eyes on me, Earl
The linguine hitteth the fan
Grounds for saturation
Flickering agendas
Bathtubs I abhor
Fast forever
Maybe yes
Or not

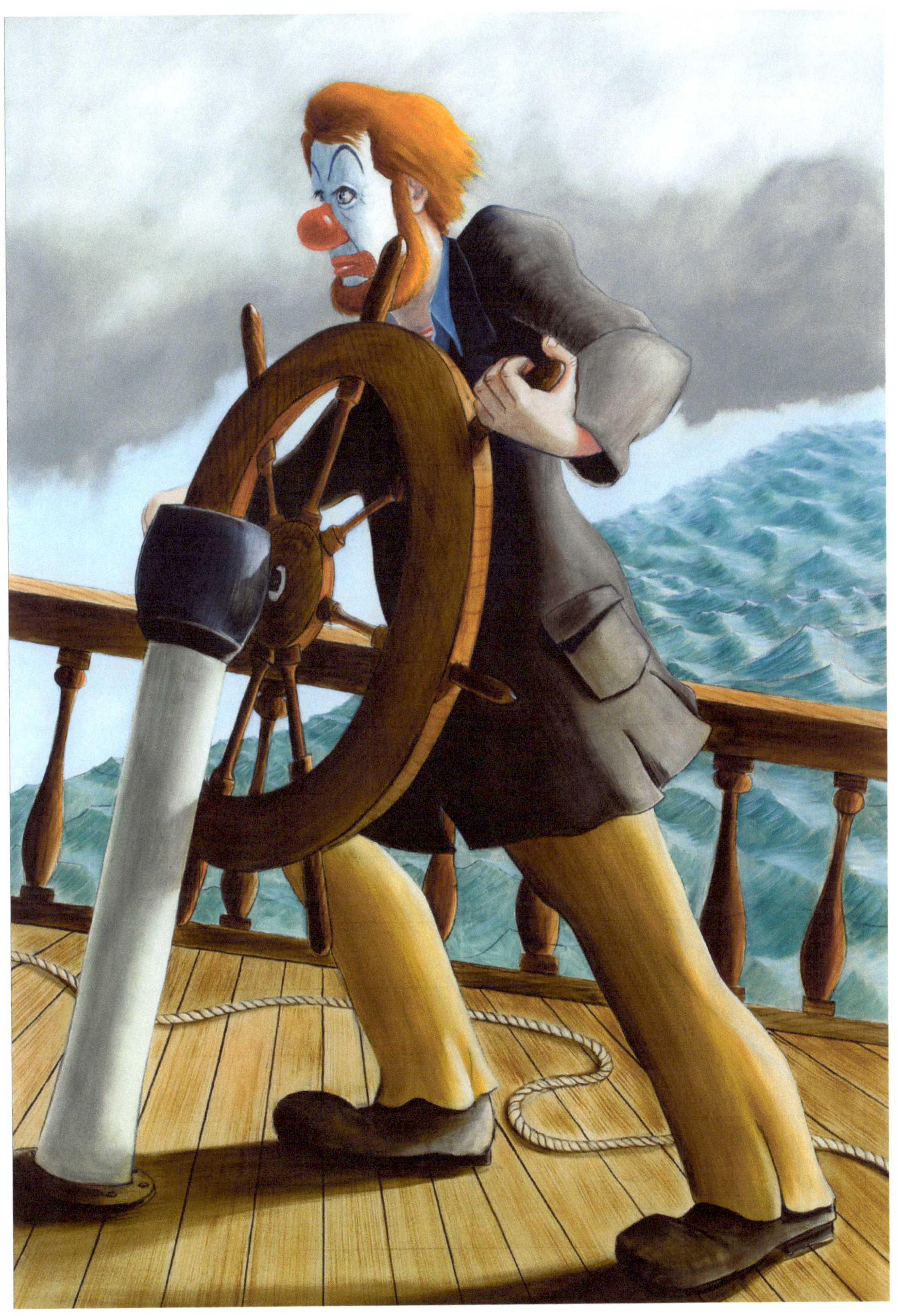

Around the World Alone (Push on Able Seaman Push On), 2011
Oil on linen, 80 x 54 in. Courtesy of Petzel Gallery, NYC

Charles Yuen

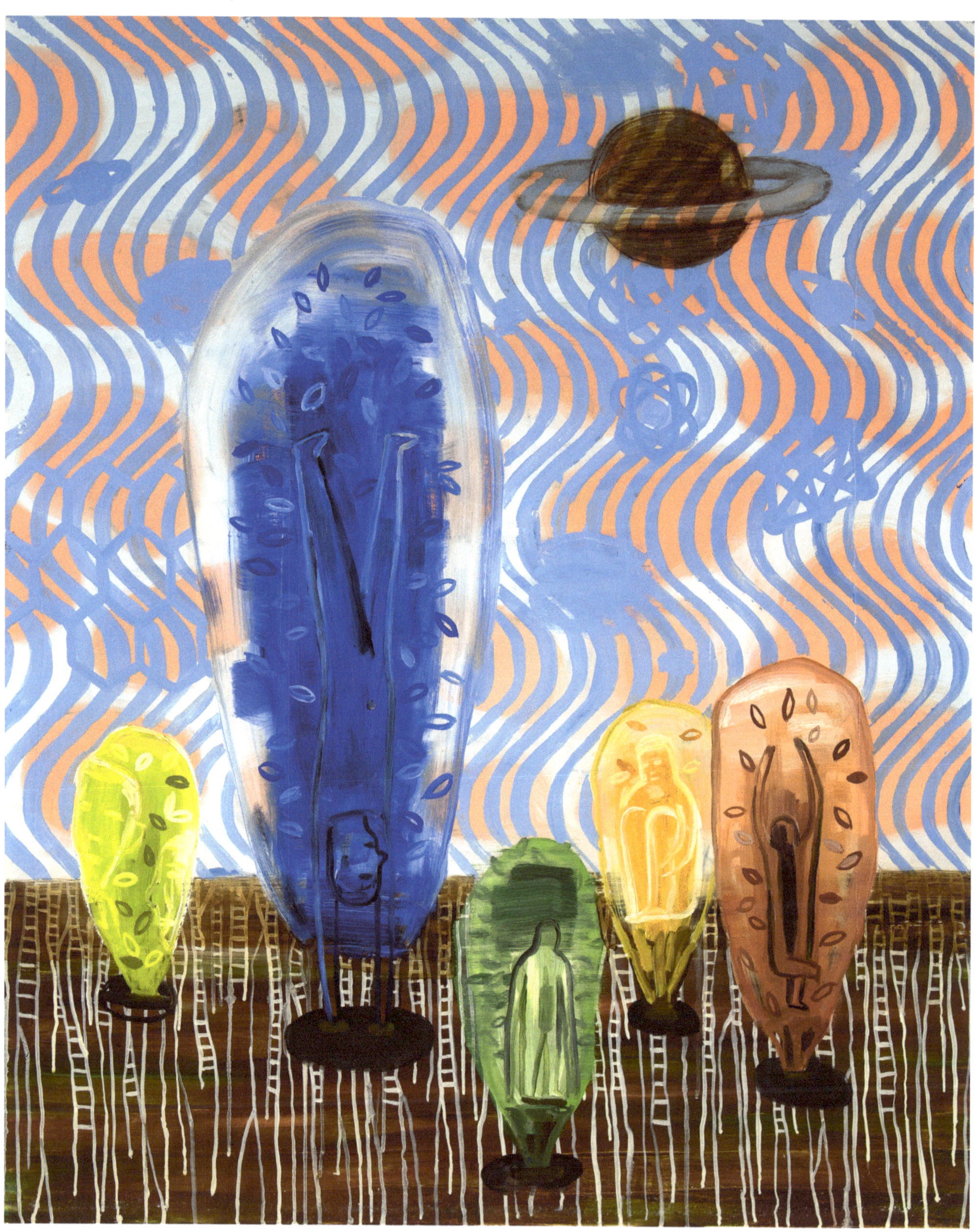

Saturnalia, 2023, oil on canvas, 48 x 40 in. Courtesy of Pierogi Gallery

July in February

Arc of the diver, curve of the bow
the way a backbone runs along the back
in sunlight something God made
a bone web that holds the beauty
upright and moves it
through the world a procession
noble as Picasso leading his glittering
entourage along the beach
beneath a giant parasol and
everyone under the sun salutes.

Catch My Breath

Holding back time like a dog on a leash
anything to slow the forward motion of the day

Music sharp as spears too many ghosts inciting
astral turbulence even the footy too hard to watch.
Word play stopped on tracks, next step must be righteous
Lovely daughter in an old Charvet shirt, they sent her out
deliberately to catch my breath, walk on my grave.
she brought me a vial of patchouli from Constantinople
that reminded me of hippie girls in Oshkosh overalls
but I had already entered the realm of the senseless.
Persephone had to spend three months of each year
underground with her father Pluto, in darkness
and gloom of night. *Wouldn't you?*

Vyt Bakiatis

Voiceover

Giddyup, you little boy!
Listen up, or I'll take away your toys.
Yours is a lifetime to enjoy,
Just pick the path that brings most joy.

With so much to say
There's no time to play.
You must write down your thoughts.
Keep a folder, and don't fret
To let yourself erase or write over.
The first thing you say should stay
In the voice spelling your future.

Borderline Link

He never crossed the line
Till he was double-crossed
Before he got there one of us
Got hauled off to slave labor
The camp we only heard about
Where high blood pressure
Felled him although he was one
Who survived having lost an eye
But that was later when he tried
Suicide before his wife grabbed
The gun away from him after
He'd collapsed and she had to
Lead him around like a dummy
By the hand and they kept
Bumping into each other like
A dance when you can't
Even hear the music

The Wound

even if it's to the heart will heal
heart's ache without showing
a scar much like spring flowers
after the height of their late-summer
crisis will fade to embrace the fall

Add-On Plus

Take a minimum of sense
Then split it in two
It's love what you get
No wisdom in view

Now you know no reason
Much better than this
To unscript kept secrets
Just to energize bliss

And envision the charm
How your countering kiss
Sets off an alarm
I don't dare to resist

So we're lucky to share
Such a pleasure as this
And long to persist
In our bliss

Beauteous One

Being Beauteous
by Rimbaud with
his title in English
keeps the mystery
ever present here
— after

You are the one Adam
Mickiewicz the great
poet who wrote in Polish
and drew from Lithuanian
legends his many ballads
the first was Grażyna
about a young woman
who roused and led
Lithuanian troops
against the medieval
Teutonic Knights

Her name was one
Mickiewicz made
up from the Lithuanian
graži means beautiful femme
by adding -na for emphasis
that became very popular
a name throughout Poland
and Lithuania thereafter

The Grażina I know
she is the one whose
blue eyes show her
face from one side
has nothing to hide
true insight and hope
to oppose the fraud
of malapropisms
that veil malfeasance

I should know
from her look
what future she'd hold
in her arms but by now
age has dulled my instinct
except her photo I've kept

Mark Vincenz

Inedible

The ferryboat smells of something approximating
Sulfur and crude oil. We stand on the jetty.
There's a gentle knocking as if the earth
Were trying to hold still. Frayed plastic bags
Float in the dockyards. I can read a few:
Bonus, Max Best, Indran's Dollar Emporium,
Cash Corner, Sanigore's Choicest Cheapest.
The stones have faces here — each of them
Minor gods cemented in, observing the mess
Of foam, spill, vegetable stalks and plastic.
The skipper draws back his mouth in an uneven
Smile, a crate of small fish in his lumbering
Hands. A red snapper stares straight through us.
On a day like this, everything keeps moving,
Everything piled under a watchful eye.

At dusk, the garbagemen pick up the remains,
Living or dead, wrapped in newsprint or cell-
Ophane, in a sheen of grease or a quiet dust

Of air.

Strangely, there's no defiant struggle, not
Even an sound. You'd expect the swell
Of angry voices, you expect the ground
To break beneath your soles, but the weight rolls
Effortlessly into larger plastic containers
Where they become the food of the future.

There's no precedence to buy and buy things
To throw into the mouth of empty space.
Someone's always dreaming of fast profits —
From the mineshafts of the Transvaal
To the sandstone quarries of the Szechuan —
Each of them digging deeper into forgetfulness.

Later, up in the mountains, the blue sea
Catches up with the night sky.

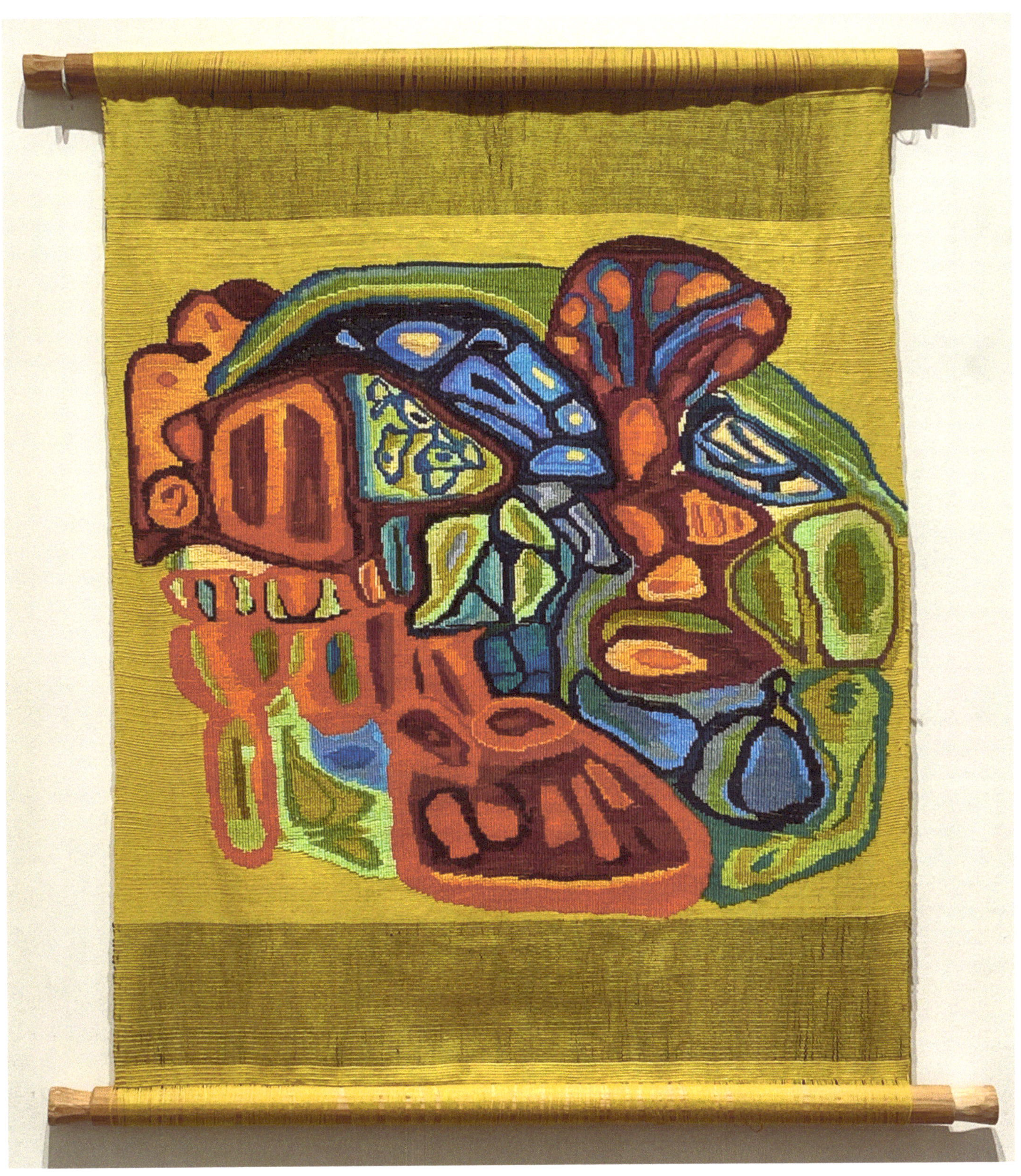

Pressure and Streams, 2023, cotton and wood, 31 x 25 in.
Weaver: María Catalina Hernández. Courtesy of Palo Gallery, NYC.

John Coletti

Rental Dog

To produce calm
become gray arrows on inner palms
relax in Tide
dust the psychic ghosts
off your eyelids
grab everyone's hands
for an hour
the ways we slide away in my life
I do it privately
w/ an abundance of care
Brandon read
his year this morning
a kind of late afternoon resurrection
in blue hearts
I misspell catalogue
all the time
but Ron says
both do the same work
staring at a copper coin
this is where I was
reading directly from the lightbulb
packing wet sandwich
into airlock
looking at my creator's
nails by the fire
the thyme on the floor is
especially pretty
a bit of mist on its lenses

Off and On

What moon is May
17 dark the night meters
clouds like abscesses
away, cover it
that poetry is psychic is no new concept
though it continues to surprise me

My Mind's Been in the Same Place Mostly

Bluebells, common dandelions
a lavender roulette chip
caffeine eyes cartoonish XXL
Kool-Aid
cherry purple. Ryman cap
copters scotched around every home's stocking keyhole
jetskis blowing against
sharp edges of bleached paper
missing being missed and other false positives
trains, molars
stimulant
panic beats while young every breath
no longer useful. I was pulled out from counting rituals screech
this possum leaps wheels
this isn't 13 living in the garage for
years w/ a hand-me-down waterbed
a velvet comforter. then parents friends' couches
gnawing diagonally across extra
archway. I let absorb
simple joy longing for a quiet debate partner, they cheer on like
outside my feet, twisted in sheets. the call for light
behind low, somber cello
hot blue
metallic crepe paper
bringing cotton candy
understanding has its joys. though it's often overrated

Mary Newell

While Stirring to Bloom

Because of nothingness, we desire to bloom.
                              after Clayton Eshleman

One hand beckons,
the other withholds.

        We stay in balance by not straying
        too far out of bounds.

Do we bloom
on this familiar ground

        where grass in passageways
        is trodden down?

Empty space pulses with photons
inclined to carry light, yet we're

        dragged toward planetary masses
        where density encumbers.

While stirring to bloom,
      probe for stillness at the root of motion,
      a vacuum that laps light in

Doors flung open,
      residuals float away
      plunge into liminal where emergence startles

Receptive to nutrient needs,
      sense air exchange from green to sanguine lives
      share the manna of compassion

Be as one   among many   becomings

Title text is from Clayton Eshleman, *Penetralia* (120).

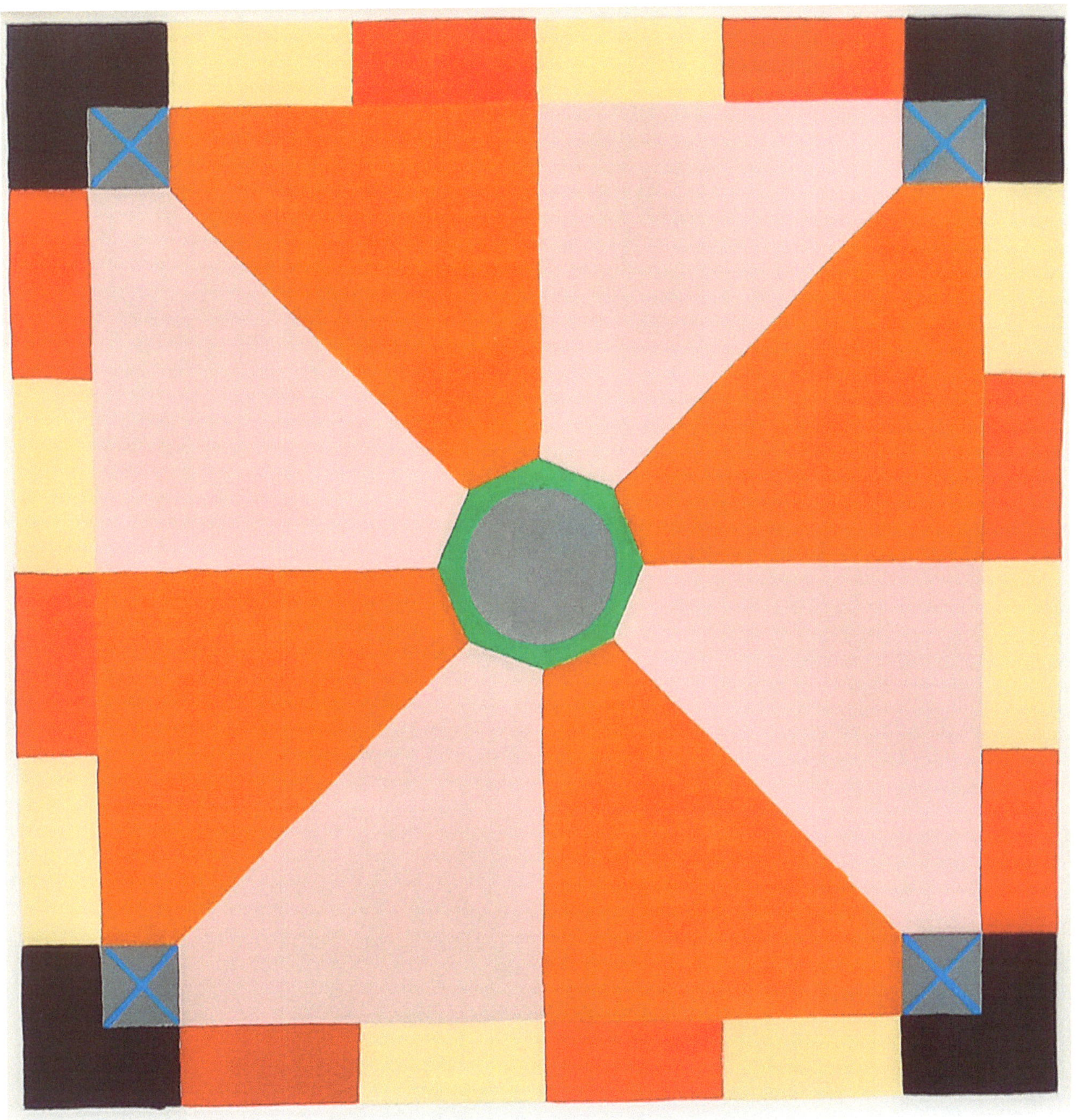

Serviette, watermedia on paper, 10 x 10 in.
Collection of Amy Galowitz. Photo: Rose Mackiewicz

Sono Kuwayama

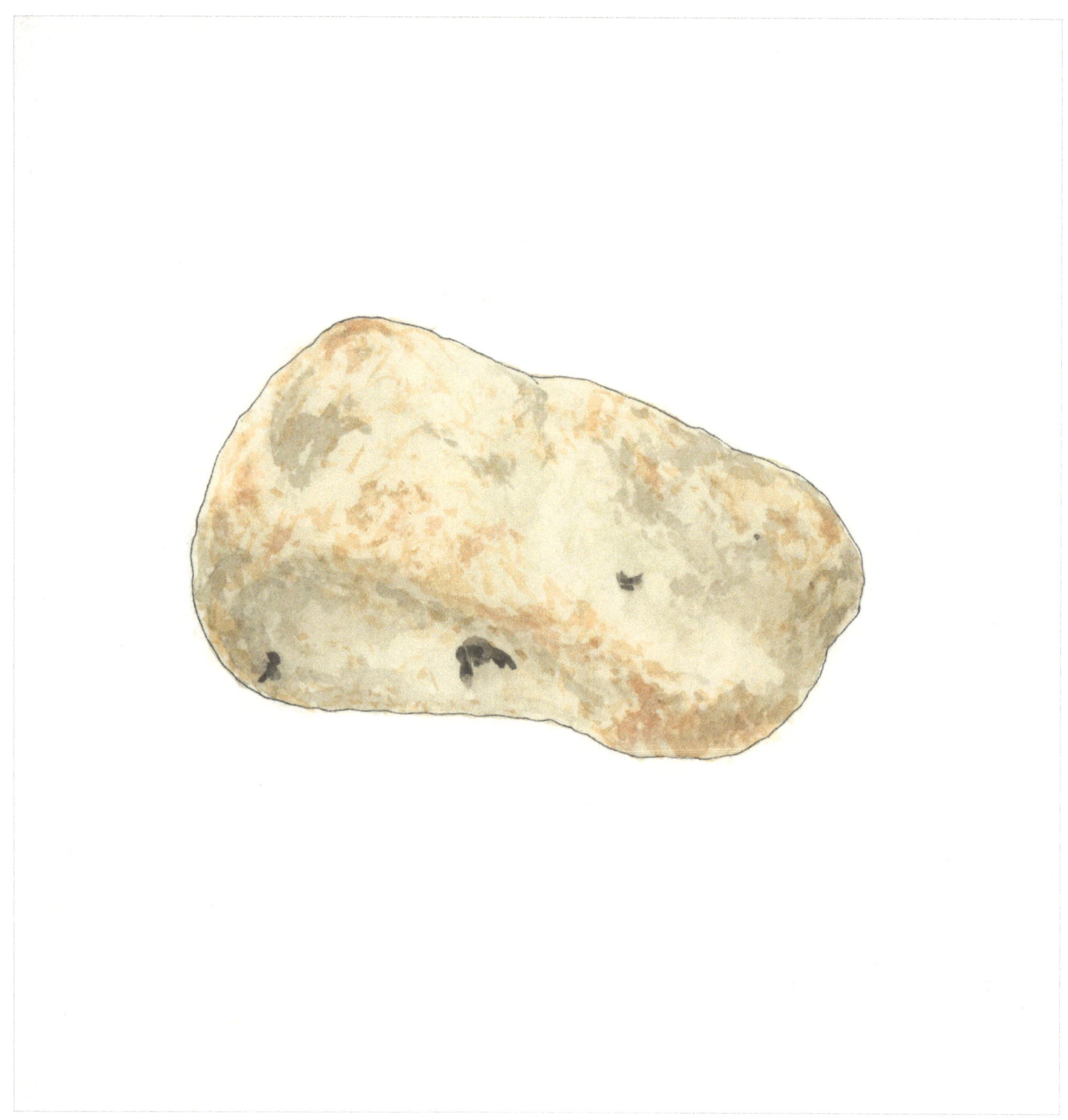

Untitled (stone), watercolor 8 x 8 in.
Courtesy Ki Smith Gallery. Photo by Roman Dean.

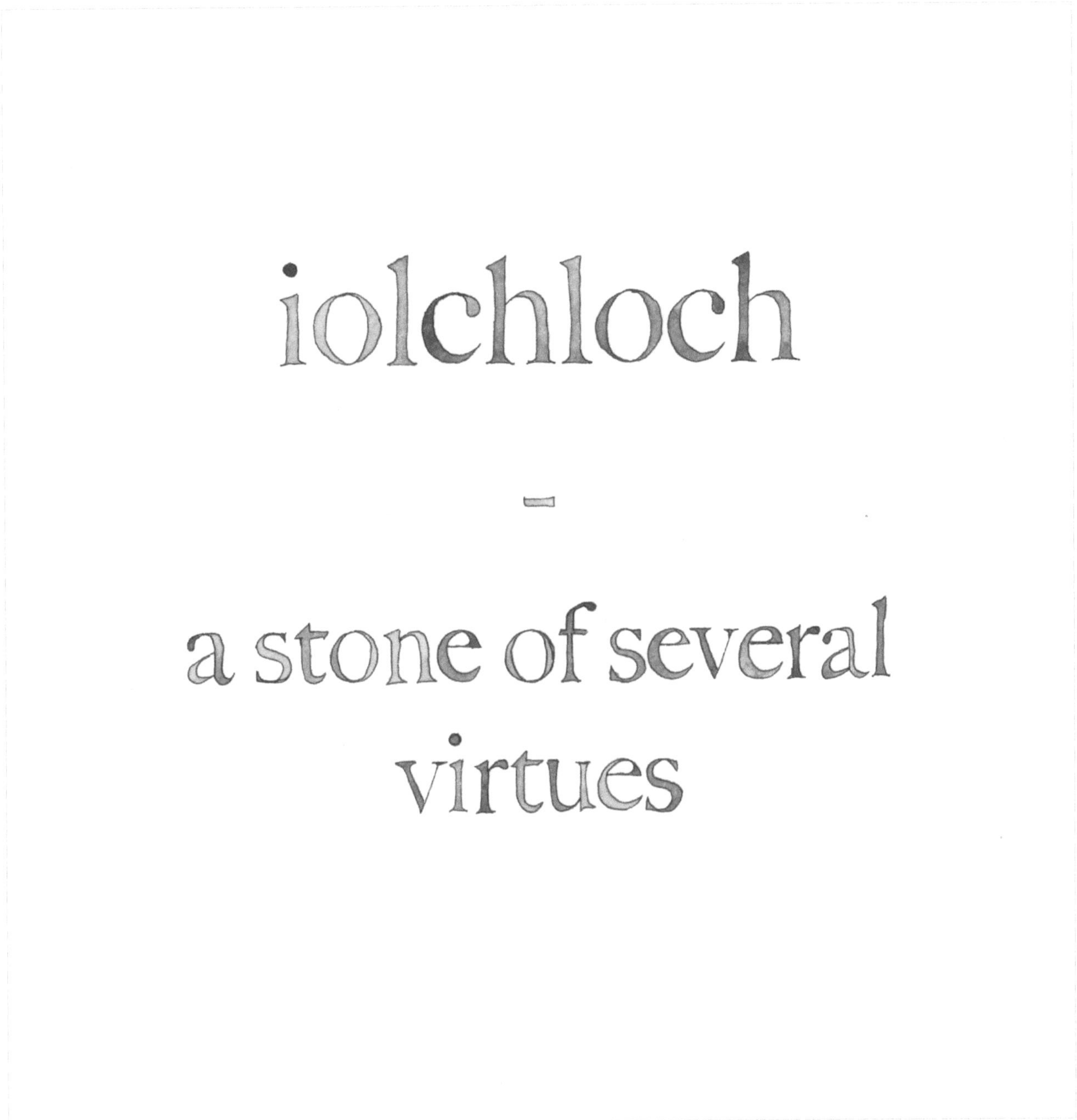

iolchloch

—

a stone of several virtues

Untitled (iolchloch), watercolor 8 x 8 in.
Courtesy Ki Smith Gallery. Photo by Roman Dean.

Leah Kogen-Elimeliah

Catwalk

I know I am not as dirty as you want me to be
but we can still re-enact a lover's match
give me a chance will you
I've got a nerve pulling at my side
and the whistle
calling me to the kitchen
like you, I might not   come —
to the level of witchery she pulled
in those days, carrying
in her treasure suitcase,
pulling tricks out from her — jesting
for me to come closer
her box full of berries smelling of ruse
of innocence of a rose
like a fairy tale she pranced around
the room — mirroring a 1920's hotel
with a bar downstairs, curtains hung
heavy — like a fairy she spinned
around in her silky 1950's baby pink
nighty, supple her body moved
with the rhythm of my hands bending
attending to her sheath - then you came
right out of the wind and snatched
that one. Covered her
in gentle touch, you
with your turned up collar
and your sway you took her away.

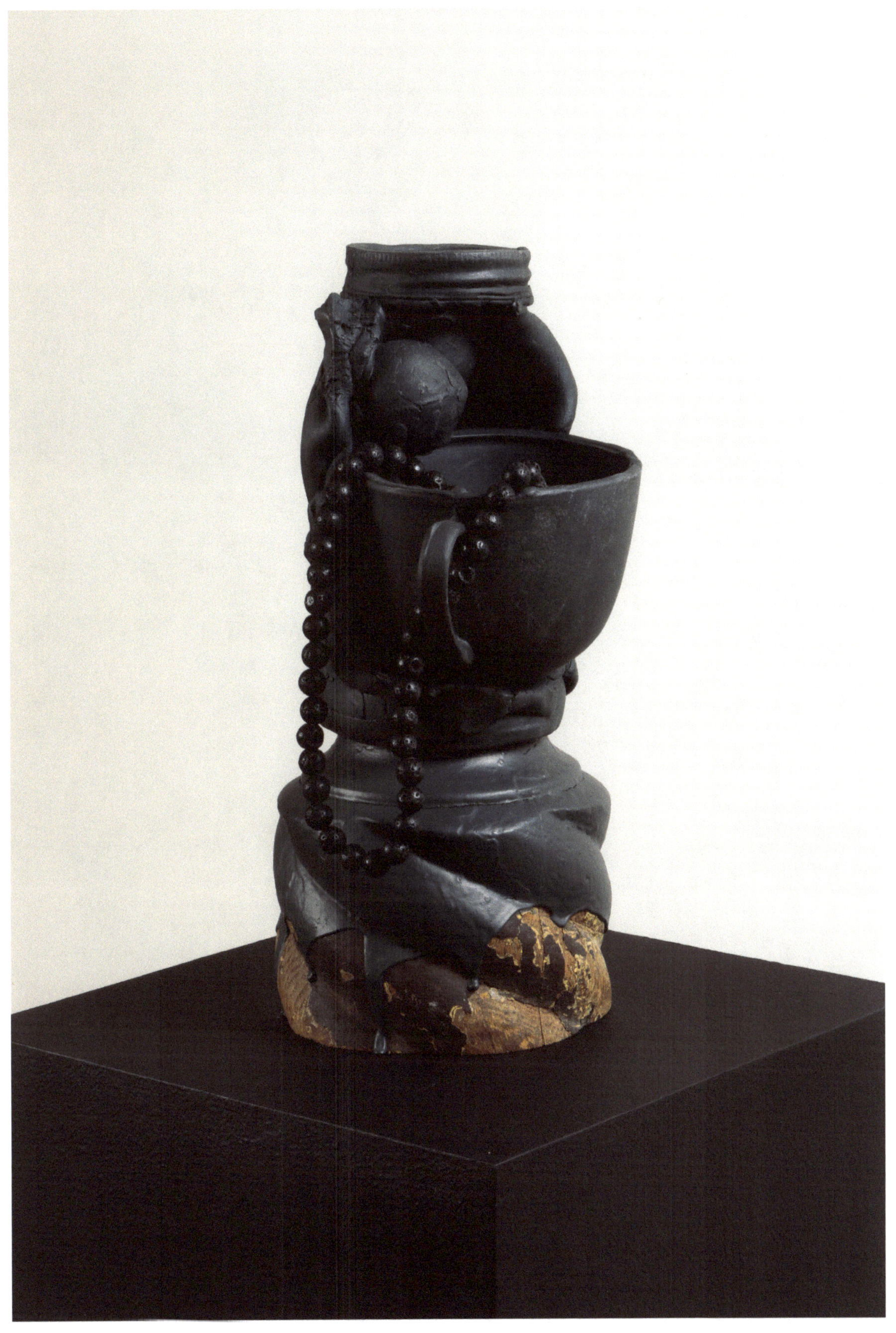

black totem 2, 2023, black porcelain slip cast, wood, lava, latex, graphite wash
9 5/8 x 6 x 5 in., © Debra Priestly, courtesy of the artist and June Kelly Gallery, NY

Danny Simmons

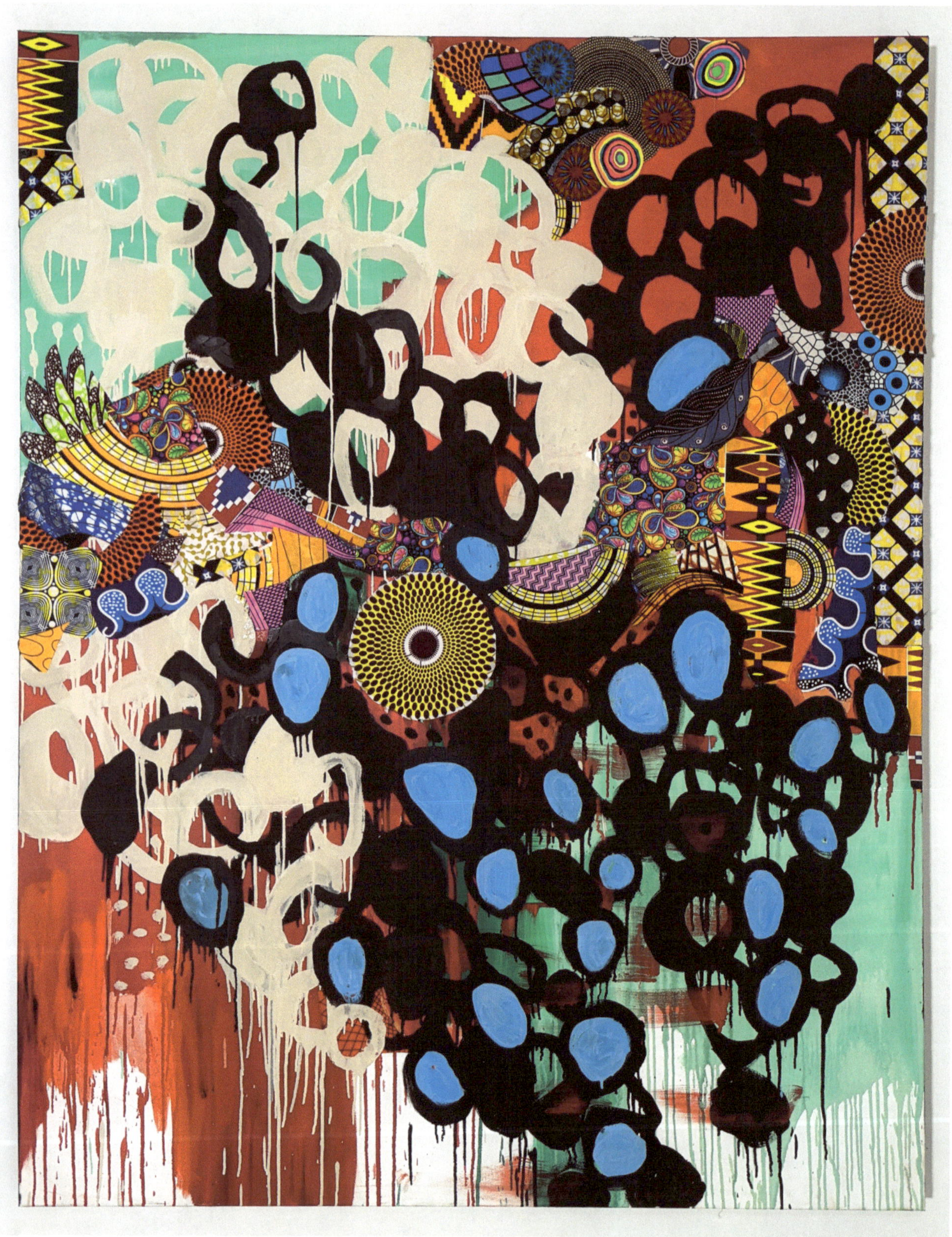

Can I Get A Witness, 2021, oil and fabric on canvas, 60 x 48 in | 152.4 x 121.9 cm.
Courtesy the artist and Westwood Gallery NYC.

You are a potato chip

who wants to be a pretzel. You are a CRV
who wants to be a red Miata. You are a man
searching his pockets and jackets and the top
of his bureau for keys. And you can't leave
until you find them. You believe you need them.
You believe the Earth is round, which is very
true, but not nearly as interesting as the Earth
is the home of unlikelihood, an unlikelihood
you don't like to look at. Who cares what you like
or don't like? This isn't a menu and you aren't
sitting at a bar. This is a poem, and so it's not wow,
you're Jesus Christ walking on water, it's wow,
you're Joe Blow walking on Earth, and yes, it is
curving slightly, which gives you your horizon,
which helps you think, so that walking thus
you realize maybe you don't need the keys or car
or bike or any kind of vehicle. You don't need
to go anywhere. You are a potato chip. You need
to just be and let yourself be eaten.

I was too lazy

to take out my notebook and write a poem.
I was too tired to utter even one word

on behalf of the universe and the way she mumbles
sleepily from the bed, protesting her

meager portion of comforter. And although
I do adjust the bedding, I am way

too whatever to describe to you the way
I'm feeling, the way dawn comes so

slowly and evenly, as if I'm living in an out
of the way diorama and the first museum

workers have just punched in and are now
turning on the lights, room by room.

Vincent Katz

Faces & Windows

I want to be alone
In this trance of lines

I don't want to reveal
Too much of myself

I'm alone among
These images

It's A Great Day

My favorite hill in the darkening
Two girls jumping in lamplight
Outside a sense of royalty

Here's another field
Soccer goals set up
On leaf-strewn field

It's a great day today
Game day and the masses
Are descending

In front of the Elmwood
All is crisp and cool
Nothing to do all day long

Still On The Corner

I'm still on the corner
We're turning 7th Ave
The car is playing dance music
At very low volume at 8:31 am

Now at Varick & Houston
My heart feels all the times
A glance toward JJ Walker
And sitting there on a bench

Now in the tunnel, now out,
In America now Love Always Wins
Says the painted mural
In blessed industrial sprawl

Far below now, miniature cars,
Highways, cylindrical gas tanks
Leveling of clouds, read, movie
Leaving and always flying

A Stroke Across Space

A stroke across space
Destroying distance
Those people spent time
Weighed on heads behind
Music lifted in halls
Opera shared recalled
And today a dull sun
Brightening is all again
Where love patters,
Somehow remains, fast
Against shutters flies
Wayward, clouds the only
Action, mind still finds
Where to swim in sky

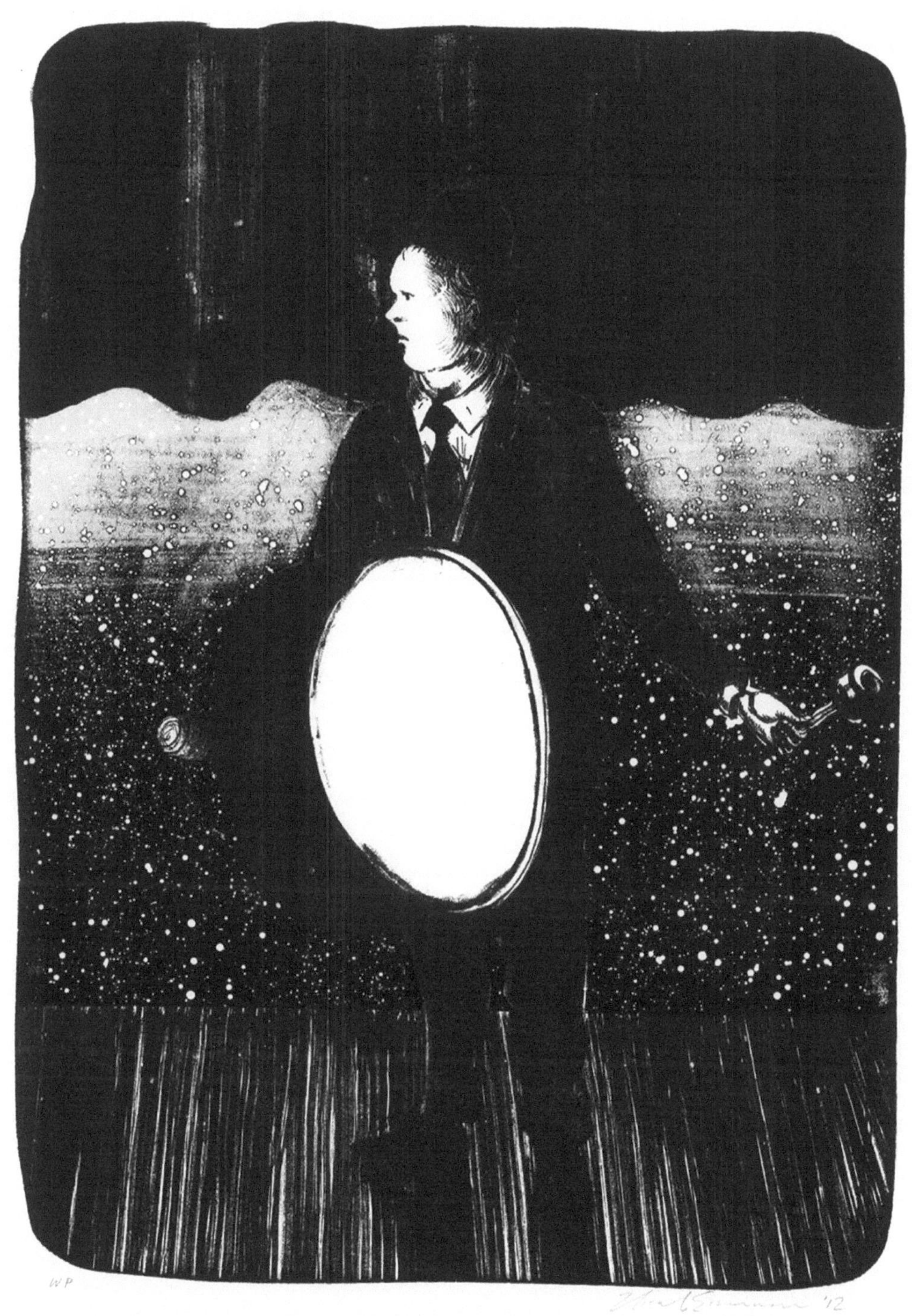

Drummer, 2011, lithograph print, 22x16¾, courtesy of Print Center, NY.
Edition of 25 by Jungle Press Editions, courtesy Jungle Press Editions. © Nicole Eisenman

Don Yorty

231

Fluttering robins louder than my singing
are violent on the lawn where they're fighting
over a worm—No!—I'm wrong. As quiet
as a junkie gets sticking the needle
in no matter what funny business
preceded it—Like a junkie suddenly
silent one bird enters the other shooting
the life force so still it makes me stop
playing to watch what I thought was a war
being fought not this sudden making love
done in dandelions and fog. The robins
hop and pull together to come apart.
As I put the guitar down, not a thought.
No sound at all but for the rain that falls.

232

My mother pulled the black snake from the bush.
Long snake gone from fleeing to being held
twined around her arm and opened its mouth
but mother only laughed and let it twist.
Her friends who had come to party at her
barbecue wanted whiskey sours, not this
and yelled "Theresa!" parting like the waves
did for Moses when his raised scepter hissed.
My mother held on through the yard toward
the house, the cellar steps, down to the dark
cellar itself. "Go, find the mice. They're yours,"
she said letting it go to the shadows
going back to her friends and the roasting corn.
That was my mother from the day she was born.

233

Life is like jumping across the rocks.
I got myself here and now I must get
myself out. Huge as a dinosaur head
and as old if not older is this rock
I'm writing on as naked as a lizard

sunning itself. The insects on my skin
have come to me or I guess I to them
though they will stay and I will go. Home's far.
I have to steady myself, be ready
not to fall, keep my balance, not tumble
into the thorns below where I'd struggle
to climb back up, knuckles numb and bloody.
Life is really like a poem and how.
If you want to get there, be here now.

234

Back at the beginning is like a dream
Back at the beginning's like waking up
Back at the beginning not everything
is formed. The pond is not a pond, it's a
big hole some giant with a shovel has dug
up. I know this place and yet I don't, yet
I know I'm home—Here is where I was born.
How do I know? Here I feel safe and sound.
Here I have flown to write and become old.
The sun's going down. Night will sing its notes.
I am what I am no matter what. I am
not able to look. Can you see my face?
Am I a bird or a man or a snake?
The stars are hid that led me to this place.

235

In many ways the tree looks like the cloud.
In many ways the hawk looks like the crow
sharing the same profile and the same form.
As the trees bend and sway out of their boughs
a long polar bear comes. Athena was
Zeus growing in size, breaking free from
his mind. I see a hawk—or's that a crow?—
on high looking down for a young swallow
to swallow. From above like an arrow
swallows point and make for the predator
who's too big to turn around and swallow
the swallows who follow with more swallows
nipping its back until it flies away.
Then in the clouds the swallows stay and play.

Rick Prol

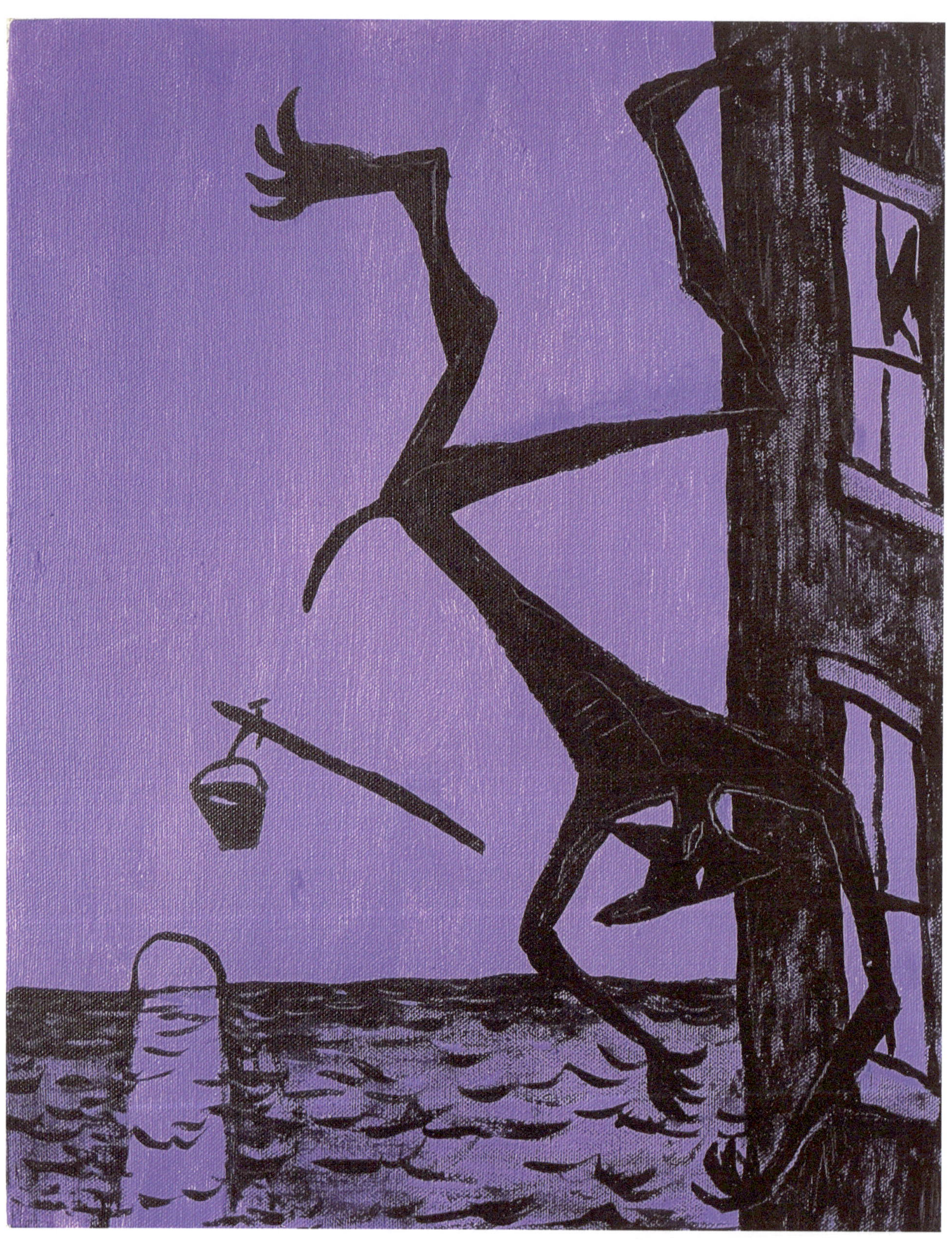

Icarus, series, 2023, acrylic on canvas, 20 x 13 in..
Courtesy of James Fuentes and Michael Klein.

Marc Vincenz

A Modern Prometheus

"There is something at work in my soul,
which I do not understand." — Mary Shelley

There was a therapeutic plan, yet at the École
You were more affected than ceremonial.

You were lavished, comfort-seeking, only
Here-and-now, and those murmurs along

The boardwalk when you sought your arti-
Ficial sleep, diving into coral reefs,

Wreathed in garlands of seaweed. Those
Were the murmurs of old beards, homage

To the ancient world tainted by carhorns.
Yes, you shouldered the planet. *Miraculous*

Really! So how does one create you?
You sat there in the Piazza, by the fountain

Feeding pigeons yesterday's bread, boys
Were leapfrogging, girls hopskotching, and

You in your head with King Lear and Cordelia.
You stared skyward thinking tragedy and

Everything dissolved into smoke and ash. Trifles
Really (but not like your Grandma made

With lots and lots of sherry and cheeries). I know
You're thinking of providing the stimulus

Package they need. If only the canal
Were less parallel we might not talk

About fantasies, instead we obey all orders,
Our noses pressed to the plateglass.

The years, if we had any, are working against us.
Or perhaps you can die twice?

Monique Erickson

Old Friends

I spent last night in Westchester, trying
to ease you through another heartbreak.
You collected me from the train station,
and we drank the fifth of Jack I mixed
with my flat Grand Central Coca-Cola.
We walked circles through the leaf-filled
drives of River Road. "I bet you haven't
seen those in a while," you said about
the stars and I nodded my head, took
a swallow from the Coke can, walked on.
I am not sure when exactly you turned.
Maybe it was the music in that white
boys' bar, or when we got down
to the vodka, or when I danced
around your living room to Elvis,
drunk as shit, and you grabbed me
by the hipbones and I did not immediately
step away. We went to sleep chastely enough,
and it was not until this morning as I stumbled
through Grand Central that I remembered
half waking in the night to your mouth mid
lick. I can't break down what you wanted
from me except maybe to remember
where a body you knew years ago
lets you slide around. Alone now
I retreat to my window seat
with my hangover and bottled water.
I accept my culpability: I wore that
short silk skirt, those cowboy boots,
I brought you the whiskey, I have
felt guilty for leaving you for years.

"People don't change," you said
as we were walking, speaking
of your girlfriend, and I agree
with you, since I am still
the girl who makes allowances
for everyone. This is not even
a good poem, what I can make
of alcohol and sex and guilt;
I am not inventing anything here:
I am not original in my shame,
nor are you, in your sorrow or your lust.

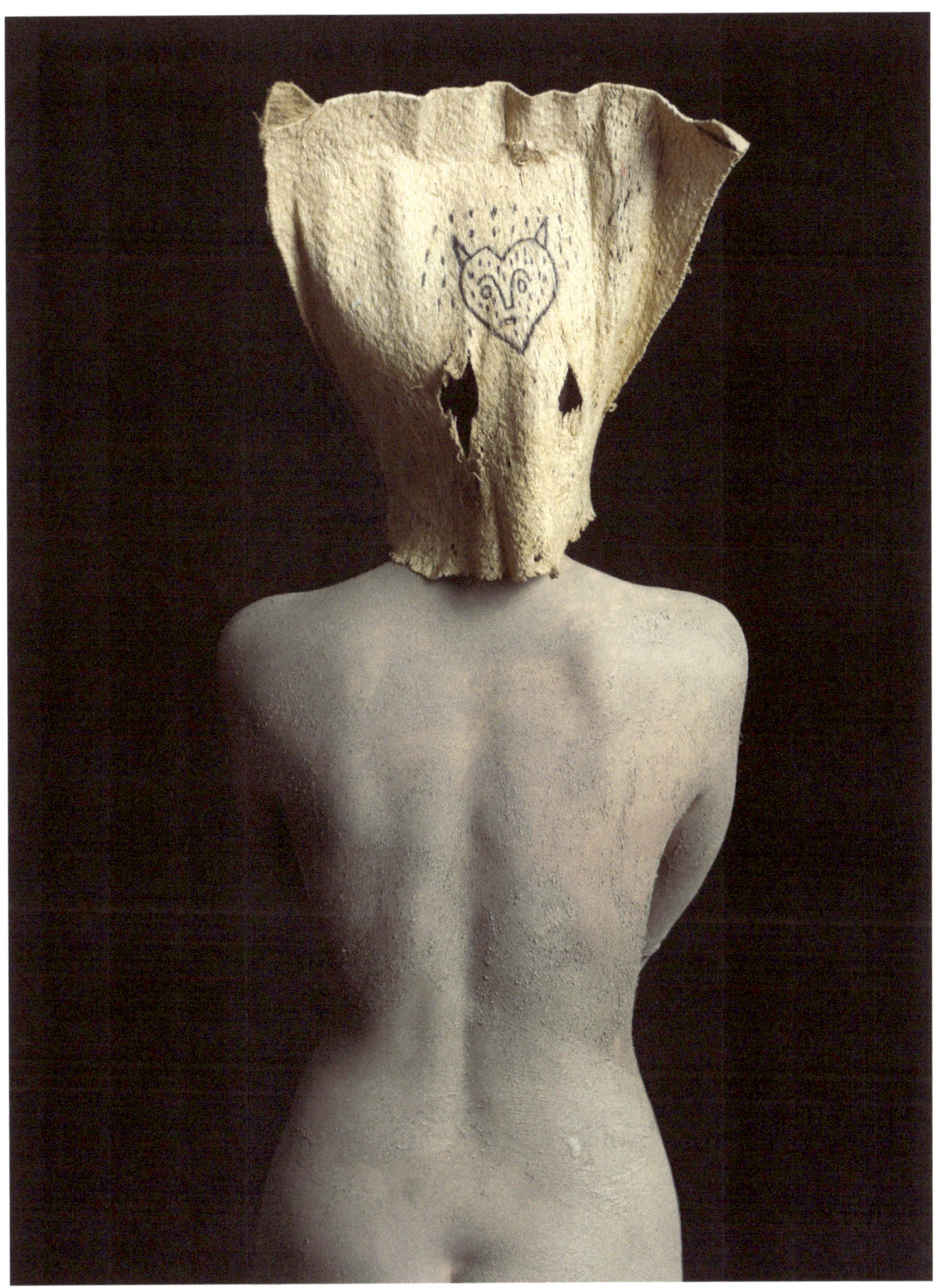

MIT 0195, 2023. Color platinum print, 31½ x 23¾ in.
Courtesy of Throckmorton Gallery.

Barbara Henning

In ’72, I’d sit at the bar in Cobbs with my book and my short beer, and I’d watch you and Allen bartending. Married to the drummer in Shadowfax, you became pregnant shortly after me. You cooked for our toddlers in Monteith Nursery, and every day you prepared and pulled their lunch and snacks to school in a wagon, along with your little girl, Esther. When Allen and I broke up, I was distraught; you came over and cleaned my apartment. In the early ’80s, you moved to the East Village, living in a third-floor walkup, floor-thru apartment, with a police lock on the door and an extra mattress in the hallway room. I stayed with you for a few weeks while looking for a job. You helped me turn an old Brooklyn tire shop into Allen’s Copy Cat, painting and building walls, a sleeping loft and counters. The ceiling is still the dark green we painted it, although now it’s an Italian grocery. You watched our dog Dorothy for a while when I was in India. With endless creative energy you made art—abstract city paintings, inside and out, collages, toy soldiers on old turntables and so on—you built stage scenery, designed clothes and hats, sold them in the street markets, opened a store, worked in the schools, taught children how to sew and make art, and planted vegetables and ran events in the Avenue B garden, and more. You were the art editor for the first issue of Long News, your collages in all five issues. For years, every Thanksgiving, I’d head over to your place for a potluck. On my fridge, there’s a button I bought at Santo’s, made by you. Whenever I open the fridge, I think of you: Welcome to McHattan.

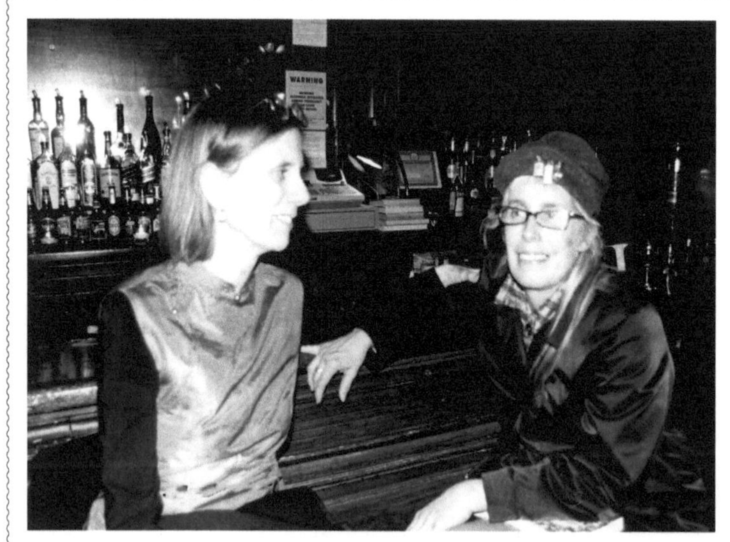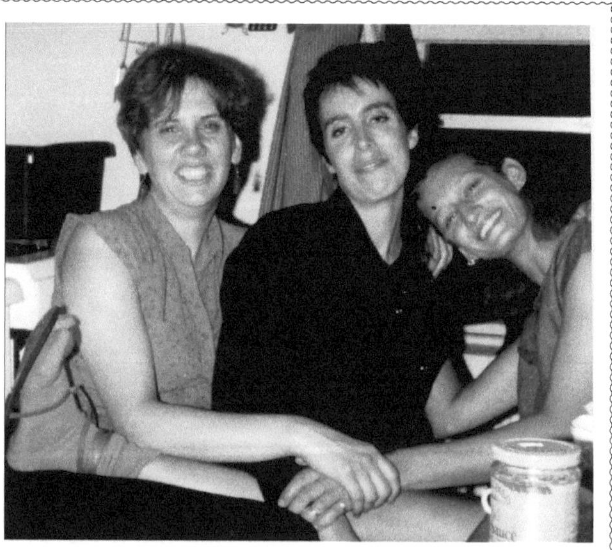

Barbara, Sally Young at KGB Bar, 2005. Photo: Cliff Fyman. R: Barb, Sally, and Raken Leaves, 1984.

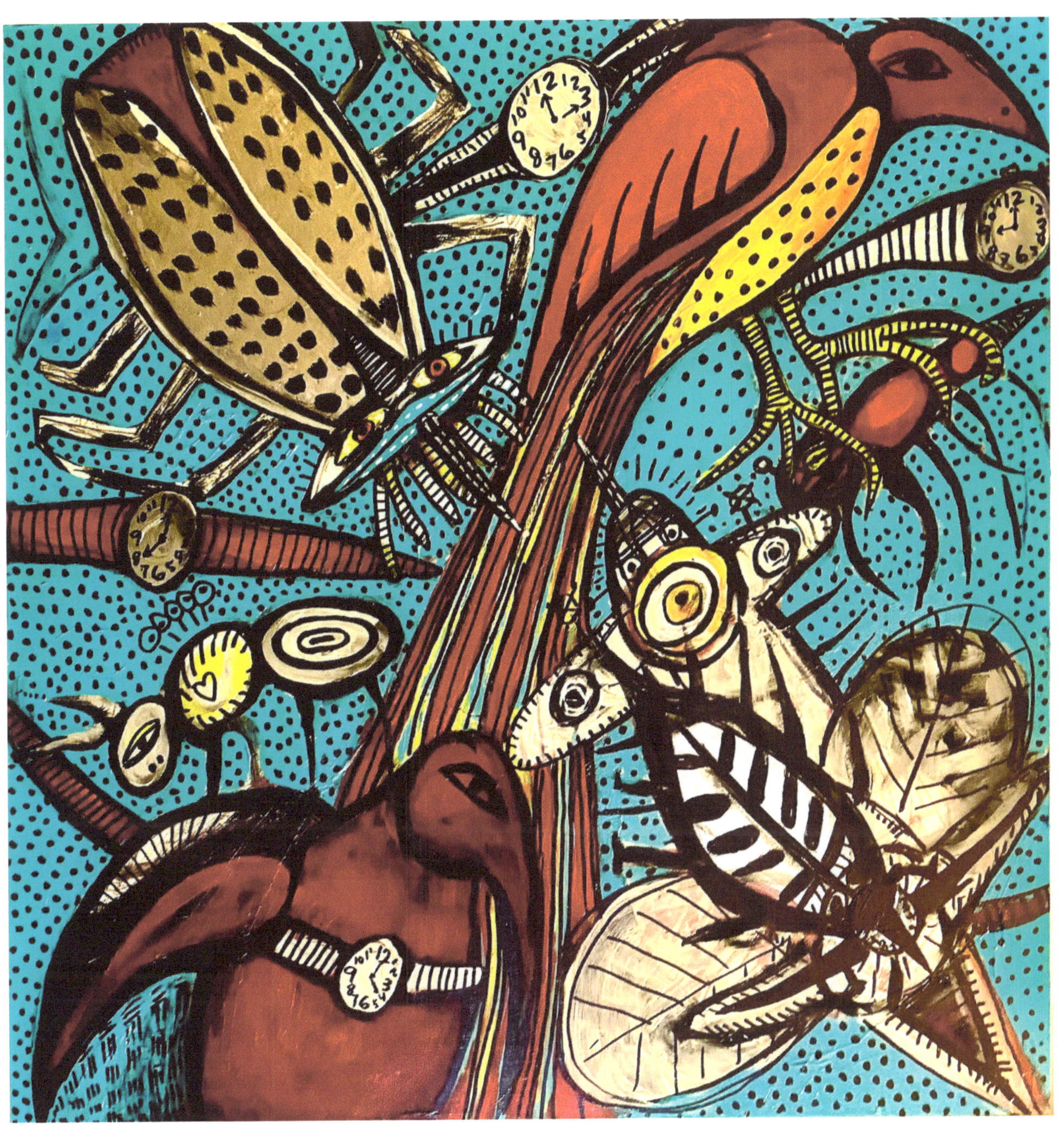

The City Under My Wing, acrylic and pen on board, 16 x 16 in.

Western Suite with a Green Sun

for Etel Adnan

Green sun
orange sky
meets blue water
at the horizon
just beyond
the foreground
yellow

—

Blue sun
yellow sky
meets blue water
at the horizon
just beyond
the foreground
salmon

—

Blood moon
Gregorian chant
meets blue water
at the horizon
just beyond
the foreground
endless debt

—

Pink moon
probably
on its way
running a few
minutes late
just beyond

the foreground
nostalgia

—

Prussian blue
television set
closed captions
for what does not
bleed yellow
just beyond
the foreground
pink stupidity

—

Clear wind
without technology
perplexed canyon
purple in last light
just beyond
the foreground
lost futures
fiber optics

—

Blue son
shades drawn
silence
just beyond
the doorway
a deserted beach
and an ocean
that does not
move

Western Suite for an
Agricultural Scene

Little blue horse
in an open field

the shape
of jazz to come

an entire world
unimagined

a complete history
of possibilities

and a future of
what if would be if

to know the being
of "thoughts"

might build
a new factory

for kindness
overnight

no matter how deeply
resonant the objects

of this particular place
have become

they aren't a part
of the world

in which the song
sings for you

Western Suite with
Five Themes
for Jim Dine

red robe
teal mallet
yellow-handled saw

blue hammer
Tricky Teeth
Nancy was appalled

red heart
a pair of gloves
onion no. 12

black eyes
New York City
Heliogravure

Rose and Grey
I've felt this way
all the way along

Brett De Palma

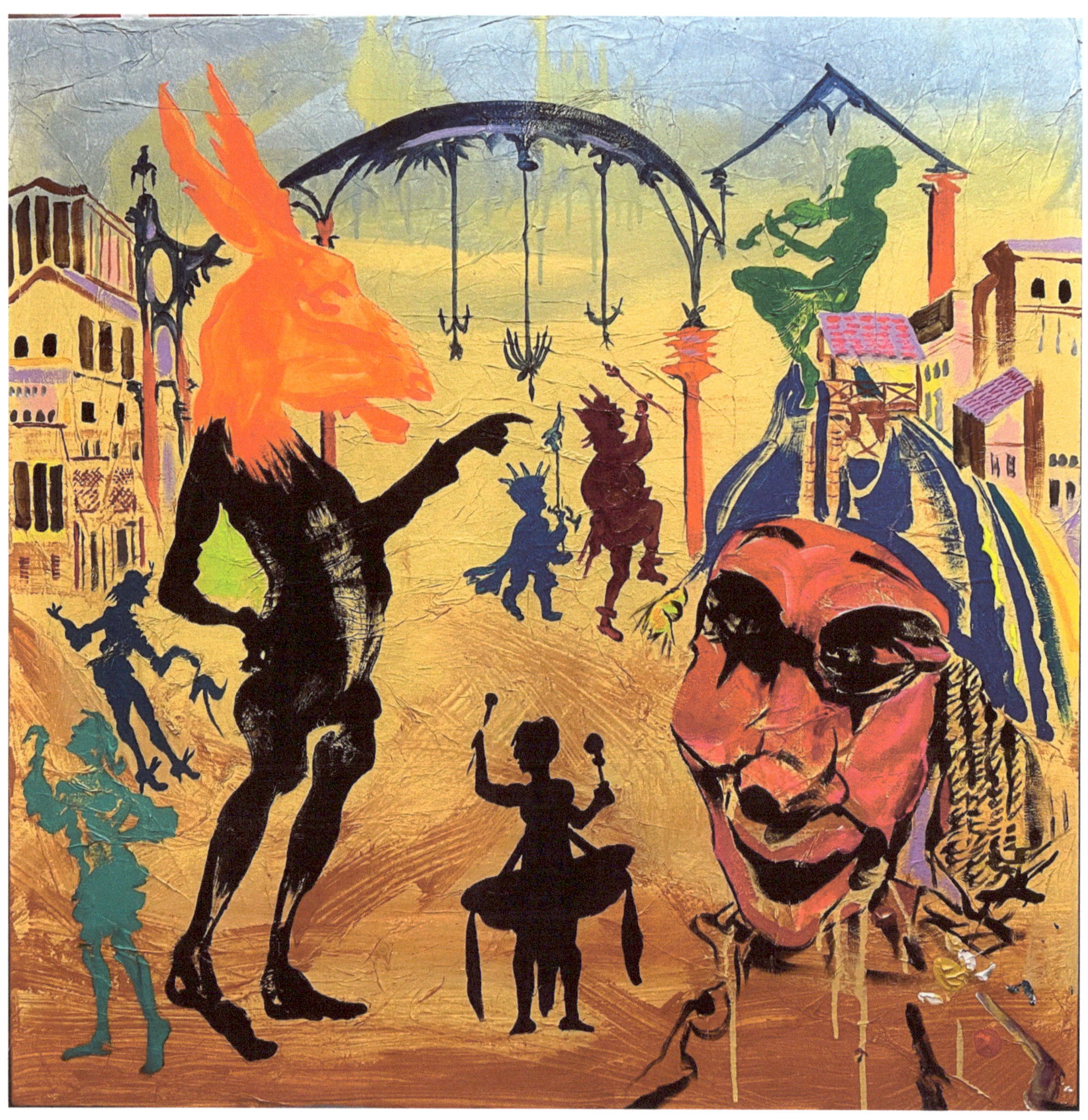

Talking Ass, 2022, acrylic on canvas, 48 x 48 in. Courtesy Howl Arts, NYC.

Contempt

Woke to an indignation of trumpets,
grand pianos sliding down a wall,
diaphanous shreds of silk
drifting like smoke on corn fields,
halos purloined from angels
shopping for their smalls
in a celestial Frederick's of Hollywood,
simian invocations
stirring the cranial gills.
the flame burns cool,
hold its beauty in your hands.

*

Indulgence confirmed
on epic summer nights
in the cornfields of the Midlands
where young girls
were removing their underwear
and you were there
you understood their sacrifice
lived among that flesh and Jabez
a prince armed with pincers
certain of nothing but your hardon
and the long days expanding
into marsupial nights
slow as beads of sweat on a dancer's lip
innocent as butter melting into
home baked bread each saintly
unsoiled moment canonized
everything impeccable
as Brigitte Bardot's ass
filmed by Godard
on the Isle of Capri,
in May of 1963.

The Magic Universe   *by Victor Bockris*

I found the Magic Universe with Andrew Wylie and Aram Saroyan in Telegraph Books. I found it in Newcastle with Connie and Tom Pickard. I found the Magic Universe in New York at William Burroughs' Bunker, I found it at Andy Warhol's Factory, I found it at Mickey Ruskin's One University Place / Chinese Chance. I found it at Andy Brown's Gotham Bookmart and Anne Waldman's St. Marks Poetry Project. I found it in Lou Reed. I found it in the photographer Marcia Resnick's loft on Canal Street overlooking the Hudson River and in the mystery of her body and mind. I found it in Joey Ramone and Arturo Vega at the Ramones' loft on East Second Street. I found it in Keith Richards and Anita Pallenberg. I found it in the Upper West Side apartment Susan Sontag inherited from Jasper Johns. I found it at my place in 106 Perry Street and in Jeff Goldberg's Traveler's Digest. I found it in the pages of John Holmstrom's *Punk Magazine* and *New York Rocker.* I found it at *High Times* and in the mind of Tom Forcade. I told him to put Johnny Rotten on the cover. He made a film about the Pistols' U.S. tour. I also investigated the film scene with Forcade. We went to Hollywood together to sell them High Times movies. This concluded with Tom wanting big collaborations with me. I was ecstatic. I had found my next Wylie. These hopes were dashed when Forcade committed suicide two weeks later.

I found the Magic Universe smoking pot in the back of a Checker Cab roaring up the West Side Highway flashing past the truck in the sky on our way to Legs and Carol's apartment, talking out of the side of my mouth like William Burroughs while Miles smiles from the jump seat. I found it in Legs McNeil. I found it in the eyes of Damita Richter at the Mudd Club and in my bed. I found it in *Negative Girls.* I found it in *The Philosophy of Andy Warhol* and in *The Third Mind* of William Burroughs and Brion Gysin. I found it in Cynthia Heimel's *Sex Tips for Girls* and Marcia Resnick's *Re-Visions.* I found it in the visual mind of Susan Williams and the films of Amos Poe, Eric Mitchel, and James Nares, Rome 78. I found it in the writing of Glenn O'Brien and Lester Bangs, in Andy Warhol's interviews with Alfred Hitchcock and Truman Capote on the Rolling Stones. In Christopher Makos' *White Trash.* I found it In the poetry of Memorial Day by Ted Berrigan and Anne Waldman. I found it in the stories of Michael Brownstein and Tina L'Hotsky and in the eyes of Allen Ginsberg talking about heroes in his apartment on East 12th Street. I found it in the beauty of Joey Ramone, who told me, "Punk is about real feelings. It's not about, 'Yeah I am a Punk and I am angry.' That's a lot of crap. It's about loving the things that really matter: passion heart and soul."

Walking up and down and through the streets of New York and working in all these places with all these people transformed me from a nervous paralyzed prick to a punk writer on the rise. I found it in the orange light that shines on the walls of the brick buildings in the West Village in the early mornings and in the late afternoons. The light we all love of the city that embraced us. And embraces us still.

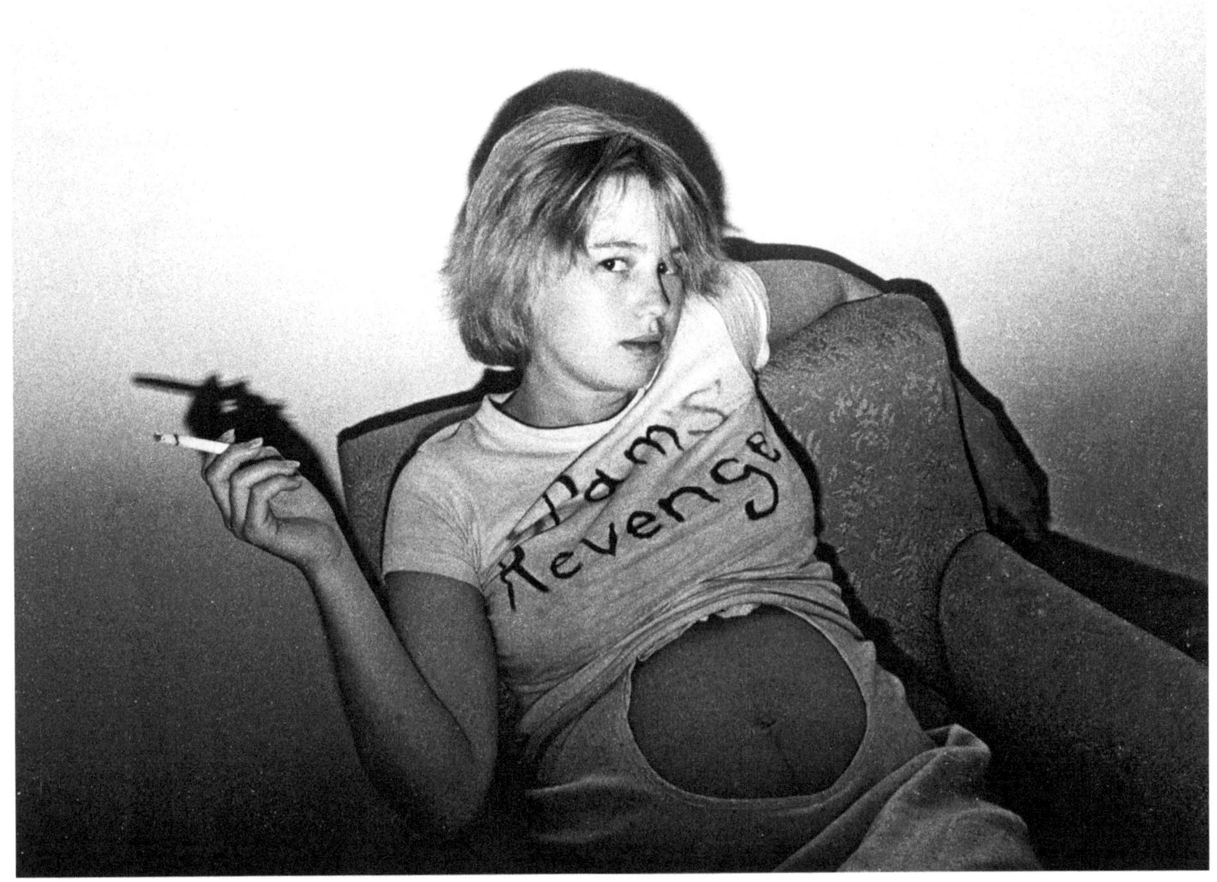

Damita Pregnant, photo: ©Marcia Resnick

When Dreams Become Realities

from The Dirty Diaries

SEPTEMBER 30, 1979

Damita brought a level of magic to those days, which matched the magic I was drawing on from Burroughs in the conversations and dinner parties we were taping for my book, *With William Burroughs: A Report from The Bunker.* In fact, it was around my talks with William about psychic sex that Damita and I found our deepest connection.

Bill and I had been on a tear-away discussion about a succubus who'd been tormenting me around the time Damita showed up. I guess the psychic sex vibes were pretty powerful. It soon transpired that not only had she had parallel experiences since she had been six but she was the first girl who ever reacted to my dreams out on the hazardous astral plane. She also had a dream in which she gave birth to William Burroughs baby. No sooner had I showed him her prose poem reporting the dream, Bill reported that his lover Ian Somerville who had died in a car crash three years earlier was stuck and couldn't find his way out. He saw her dream as a possible opening, which was doubly amazing since Bill rarely if ever let girls into his magic universe. Meanwhile, Bill and I were arguing about the reality of dreams. I pinned him on the difference between dreams and reality. "Oh really?" he replied, drawing himself up like a prim Victorian governess, "How would you define the difference?"

"In dreams if somebody hits you, you don't have a bruise in the morning."

"Oh don't you? That's not true at all, my dear. I've woken up with a black eye."

The following night I did a terrible thing that would get me into serious trouble down the line. I had fucked Damita into a limp rag doll and left her with her panties around one ankle and one knee sock ripped off. Now she lay beside me in repose like a cat. All I can say is I guess she turned me on so much that afterwards I had to go elsewhere to satisfy myself. And so I started having powerful sexual fantasies about the other promiscuous little siren whose pert body drove me wild. The problem was I forgot that Maryjane fantasies always catalyzed the succubus. I had never before summoned the succubus when somebody else with whom I had already had sex was lying there unconscious and unable to defend themselves from my selfish and thoughtless betrayal. Next thing I knew, I heard the ominous beating of the wings that heralded the arrival of the demon as it landed on my back.

I lay on my stomach pinned to the mattress unable to turn around and face it, desperately trying to expel whatever was attempting with a tremendously ferocious drive to invade the space between us and take me for herself. In the instant that I succeeded and the spirit lifted off me I spun around and lay on my back breathing heavily, freaked out by what I had done. At that precise moment Damita sat bolt upright to my right, breathing heavily. I knew as if connected by shared electrons without words that her breathing movement was a reaction to mine.

"What happened," I gasped.

"I was trying to leave a party or some gathering on a high floor," she told me urgently. "They wanted me to leave. It was as if I was being thrown out and I was scared. I ran to the elevator and ran in trying to get away from the people, but two of them followed me in and pushed a button. The elevator started going down, then it started falling out of control, faster and faster hurtling down. I was thrown down to my knees and I could not move. I knew if it crashed I would die ... I was trying so hard to wake up." She was terrified. I knew it was my fault.

I got up and turned on the lights and got her a glass of milk. I had been told this was how to break the connection with the nightmare. I sat down and comforted her. That was when I noticed that Damita had a small bruise on each of her knees. She was really terrified and I felt horrible like a driveling idiot. I didn't think I was the kind of person who would play so fast and loose with somebody else's safety on the astral plane. I was clearly not in control of what I was doing. I made her look me in the eye and I made her promise that from now on, to wake me up whenever she woke up alone in the night.

And I promised her, I said, "I will make sure you're safe, and I will stay up and watch over you so you can go back to sleep."

By then I knew a lot more about her life. I was beginning to understand why she was so afraid, and why she used sex as a way to get men to take care of her. As I lay awake listening to her breathing I stretched across and caressed Damita's hand. It took me several seconds to register that the hand I was holding was not Damita's, but a slender, slippery, long fingered thing. It was an icy cold wet and disgustingly slimy thing grabbing my skin.

Victor Bockris

Victor Bockris & Marcia Resnick

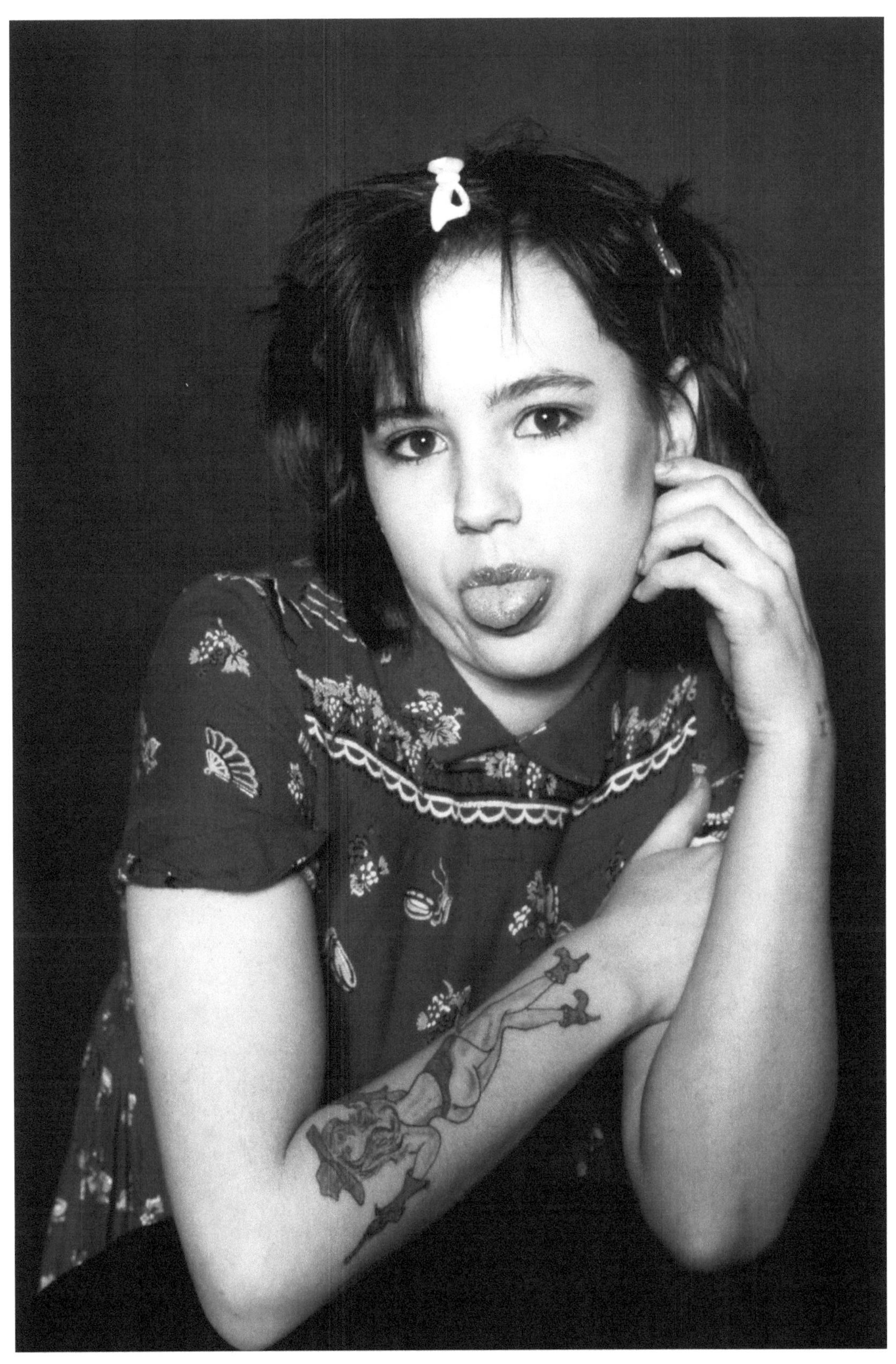

Damita with Tongue, photo © Marcia Resnick

Wanda Phipps

The Pendulum

she said "I have to get my
pendulum away from my kids
no one's supposed to touch
your pendulum but you —
now I have to re-purify it
with either
sunlight or moonlight
and invest it with
my energy"
she held up the little
inverted golden pyramid
with a cone shaped golden
spiral flowing up from it
all dangling from a gold chain
it swayed back and forth
"for divinations that require
yes or no answers" she said
as I watched the swaying
golden spiral bringing to mind
the golden ratio and
the fibonacci sequence
appearing so often in nature
a conch shell expanding
and multiplying
into infinity
she pulled the oracle card
called mama killa
the incan goddess of the moon
who governs all cycles
the seasons, cycles in life
projects, relationship
the message: know your intentions
wait for the divine cycle
to play out
wait
until the swaying
pendulum
stops

Mirror, Mirror

by Lori Ortiz

I recognize Maureen McQuillan's mid-century palette in her solo show of new work: process printing colors; technicolor; and muted, natural tertiaries blend in layers like stacked sheets of translucent, differently colored Plexiglass. She blends with glazes, arriving at a multitude of hues, as color field painter Morris Louis did by overlapping thinned washes.

Her paintings' lustrous, glassy surfaces are immediately alluring. While their shine is reflecting, they take us into their depth of about a half-inch of resin-like acrylic, treating us to watery-looking environments. Diaphanous elements that repeat, fill the panels end-to-end, intimating infinity. Her measured spacing of these forms adds geometric rhythm.

McQuillan distributes her colors into layered, clear acrylic over black panels, incorporating opaque white lines. All of this coalesces optically. To some degree she lets the materials do their thing. Their chemical action generates some of the imagery.

The paintings' mirror-like gloss helps us personalize the viewing experience. Forms emerge from the matrix, suggesting stacks of wine glasses that recede rows, portals, DNA or other intimations of mother nature. The green-tinted elements' curvy outer edges are like kelp fronds ruffling in the ocean.

McQuillan is posing opposites in the yin vs. yang of softly-pooled, colored veils,

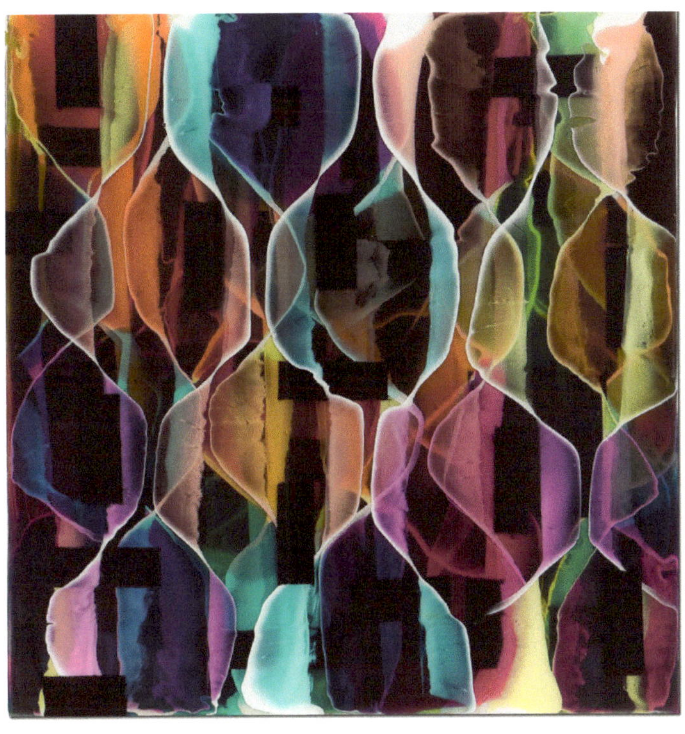

Untitled (TW/O/3B), 2020, ink and acrylic polymers on wood panel, 10 x 10 in., courtesy of McKenzie Gallery, NY

MAUREEN MCQUILLAN: TWO WAYS ABOUT IT AT MCKENZIE FINE ART

in curvilinear life-like forms that butt against opaque black shapes or stop at sharp white borders. The optical *weave* of twisted, wafer-thin ribbons in the substrate plays against the *warp* of static posts, deep dark backgrounds, or voids in time and space. These black, hard-edged rectangular patches give the whole a gravity. They add a code of redactions, pulling back the sweetness. They are harbingers of something amiss, disrupting the natural flow.

The works invoke compassion, for example: for the lives of pregnant women and for the environment. Because that's where we (still) are in 2024. McQuillan's conceptual intelligence and rigor becomes evident the more we look and think about these layered works, even as their sheer beauty feels life-affirming.

END RUN

Fun, thou art our weapon. Courage, our boon.

We've made it to issue #20 thanks to our team: designer and contributor Lori Ortiz and Deputy Editor Ilka Scobie. Thanks to those who have supported us over the years beginning with Bob Holman's initial offer in 2007 to to do a gig at the Bowery Poetry Club.

This year we celebrated five years of collaboration with Jane Friedman and Howl! Marcia Resnick, Walter Steding, Penny Arcade, Sono Kuwayama, and others presented work at our party. We also held our annual publication party at La Mama featuring Charles Yuen, Wanda Phipps and others from the issue. Thanks William Electric Black!

Tompkins Square Library hosted an afternoon of readings with John Yau, Elaine Equi (who included me in *Best American Poetry 2023*, from Scribner's, thank you big time!) and me.

And Jefferson Market Library hosted an evening to celebrate issue #19 with artists Emily Cheng, Judy Simonian, and Patricia Fabricant. Another evening there we screened the biographical film about me that Luigi Cazzaniga made, a commission by librarian Alyona Glushchenkova.

With readings by Greg Masters and Monique Erickson who has just published *Lonesome Magazine*. I'll be showing the film this year at my undergrad alma mater West Virginia University, which is home for my archives.

Lit Balm, the zoom poetry series Marc Vincenz began four years ago, is still running strong. I've become a co-host and am booking some afternoons. Readers I've invited include Terence Winch, Annabel Lee, Kim Lyons, Vyt Bakaitis, Billie Chernicoff, Lydia Cortés, Brenda Coultas, Mark Statman, Joanna Fuhrman, and David Shapiro.

Marc also runs MadHat Press which brought out my book of sonnets and artwork, *Doppelgängster, Portraits in a Fun House Mirror.* Thanks Adeena Karasick and Leah Elimeliah for hosting publication parties! And thanks Jim Feast for the interview in *Rain Taxi.* I also read in a *Brooklyn Rail* series with artist Sean Landers. Thanks BR series coordinator, Chloe Stagman.

Pepón Osorio's retrospective at the New Museum showed off his genius for assemblage and installations. Likewise, Pablo Delano, a sypmatico

Fotobooth picture of JCW, Greg Masters, Maggie Dubris at Otto's Shrunken Head reading organized by Linda Kleinbub.

Let us forward then, and torches bring!

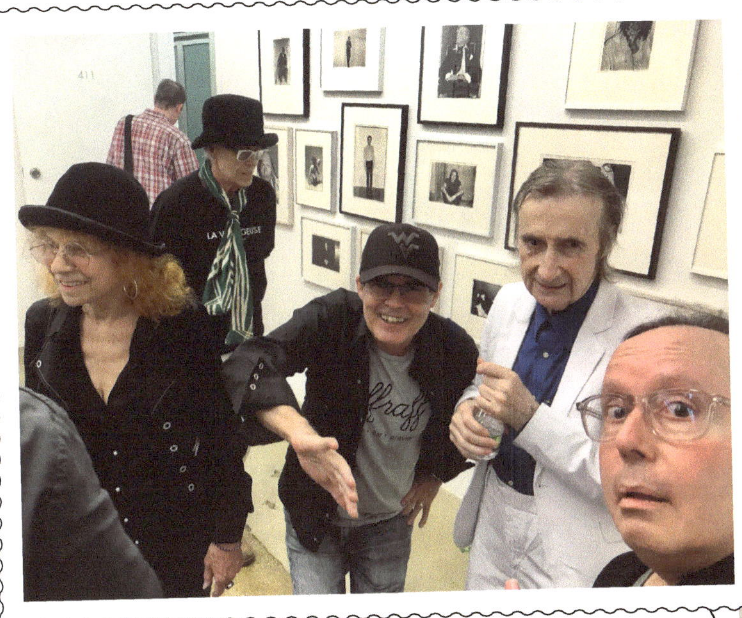

artist who shares Puerto Rican roots, expanded on precepts he developed in "The Old Colony Musuem" with a book and shows. I was thrilled to review both artists for *ArtNexus*. Pablo will be in the 60th Venice Biennale!

Now working on *Erato's Inbox* with poly-artist and publisher Barbara Rosenthal. Watch for the New Romantic poem in book form with AI interpretive artwork. We previewed the work at the BronxArtSpace.

Finally, *Fuel for Love*, my 20th book, is just out from SurVision Press, having won the James Tate Award in Poetry. Thanks Publisher and Editor Tony Kitt! Torch On!

JCW

L; Photo by Ronnie Norpel

L-r. Barbara Rosenthal, Bernd Nabr, JCW, Victor Bockris, Bobby Grossman at Deborah Bell Gallery for Marcia Resnick opening.

R: Photo by JCW

Lori Ortiz sallying behind one of Martha Rosler's installations of work from the '60s and '70s at Mitchell-Innis & Nash Gallery.

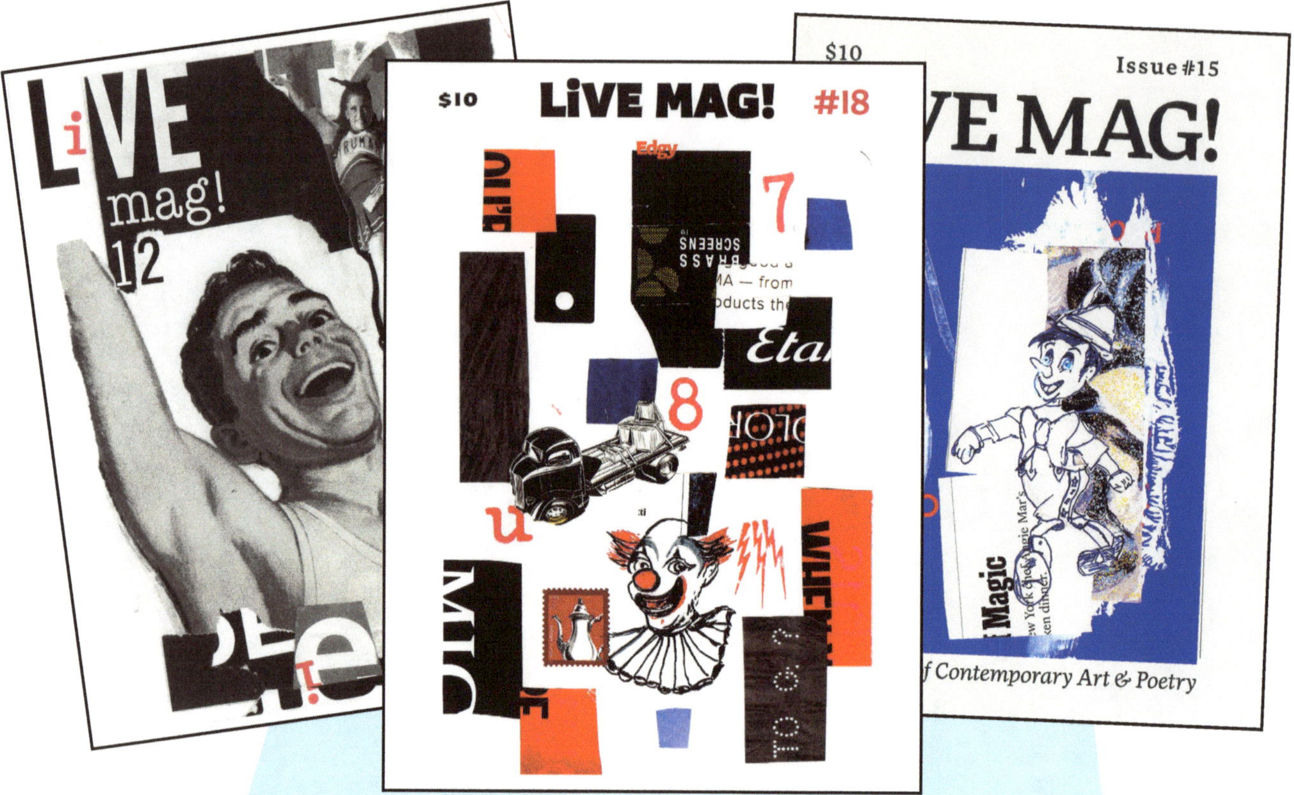

LiVE MAG!

From the stage to the page, from the wall to
the journal—each exciting issue is filled with
contemporary art and poetry. Snazzy, snappy,
and savvy—order a copy of Live! TODAY!

Small editions and rare back issues with hand-embellished covers .
Order directly from Live!
Issues also available from Ingram/Spark.

https://store.livemag.org